Defining Teaching Excellence

The Characteristics, Practices and Experiences of Highly Effective Teachers

Dr. Keith E. Leger

DEDICATION

This book is dedicated to Anna Mae Primeaux (1921-2011), my loving and angelic Maw-maw. Her genuine and unconditional love for all of her family is unsurpassed. She provided a simple, yet profound, set of guidelines for living a righteous life through her daily examples. I can still sense the love she expressed by helping us get ready for school in the morning, singing, "School days are here again! Happy days are here again," and then welcoming us back in the afternoon with a slice of icebox pie. Despite completing only the sixth grade, she emphasized the importance of "getting a good education" and I can still hear her say in that soft, sweet, Cajun-French voice, "Go to school and learn, t-babe." She made all of her grandchildren and great-grandchildren feel like each of us was her favorite. Her faith in God and belief in me to do good things and live a wholesome life continues to inspire me.

TABLE OF CONTENTS

The results of numerous studies have shown that experienced, highly effective teachers are the single most influential factor affecting student achievement today.

understanding

thinking

empathetic

rapport

routines

organized

improvement

fun

expectations

genuine

structure

energy

respect

reflection

enthusiasm

engaging

feedback

consistent

procedures

meaningful

attitude

activities

humor

student-centered

facilitating

caring

management

hands-on

communication

smile

passionate

positive

interesting

planning

reinforce

compassion

student-led

prepared

ACKNOWLEDGMENTS

To my extraordinary, intelligent, and beautiful wife, Jennifer who is unconditionally supportive of my projects, endeavors, hopes and dreams.

To my children, Marques, Joel, Angelle and Beau whom I love more than they can ever know.

To my parents, Eddie and Jeanette for providing a safe, happy childhood and home in which education, high character, morals, and dignity were instilled. I am who I am today because of the foundation they laid.

A sincere thank you to the ten teachers who shared their stories with me and serve as the basis of the study. I continue to be in awe of your accomplishments and dedication to your students and the education profession. It was truly a joy to get to know you. It is my hope that your comments, practices, experiences, and ideas will assist other teachers in becoming highly effective as well.

And finally, but no less important, a heartfelt admiration and appreciation to all of my teachers as well as every teacher with whom I've worked.

PROLOGUE

The information and quotes in this book are excerpts from a doctoral study and respective dissertation conducted and written by Dr. Keith Leger. The study was designed to identify and describe the common characteristics, experiences, and practices of teachers with perfect evaluation scores.

The findings, emerging themes and implications are universally applicable to anyone in the K-12 education profession. Pseudonyms have been assigned to the participating teachers who were purposefully selected from schools with varying socioeconomic demographics as well as various geographic regions in the state.

Using a narrative interview process, data were collected and analyzed from 10 teachers who earned a 4.0 on their respective observation rubrics and a Value Added Model (VAM) percentile ranking of 80 or above. Results of the study revealed the characteristics, practices, and experiences of highly effective teachers who have earned the highest possible evaluation score.

After analyzing the results, emerging themes pointed to a set of common characteristics, practices, philosophies, and traits. Findings from the study suggest that highly effective teachers are genuinely caring, organized, and content knowledgeable. They facilitate meaningful activities, assess content mastery and orchestrate student-centered classrooms.

1 WHAT IS HIGHLY EFFECTIVE TEACHING?

Participants identified the following emergent themes as characteristics and descriptions of highly effective teaching. Findings suggested that highly effective teaching means that teachers are engaged in facilitating fun, interesting, and meaningful activities, possessing a high level of teacher energy and enthusiasm, exhibiting high expectations, emphasizing high order thinking skills, maintaining an organized classroom that has consistent, structured, student-led routines, and exhibiting genuinely caring, compassionate, empathetic and fair concern for students.

Facilitating fun, interesting, and meaningful activities.

Nearly all participants expressed the importance of creating a fun learning atmosphere in which activities are meaningful and perceived by students to be interesting. When asked how she ensured that all students are engaged, Ms. Miller emphasized the key was in keeping students' attention by incorporating a variety of interesting and fun activities in her lessons with seamless transitions. She elaborated:

> I try to spend a minimal amount of time on each topic so that they're always moving to different activities because when you're lecturing for 30 minutes, they start dozing off. I use activities in which they move, not just their hands, but their body as well. Getting up and moving to the next desk or doing a jumping jack or something that has them moving has an effect on keeping them engaged. I like making the activities fun. They like to laugh and I like to laugh too so we tell some science jokes. I tell them stories about my kids, we laugh and joke and that keeps them engaged.

Ms. Lane commented that her students would describe her as "someone who is funny but strict." She expounded, "They want someone who makes learning fun, interesting, and applies lesson content to their lives." Ms. Turner explained, "The way you present the information has to be fun because you're dealing with a techie generation." She added, "I'm not techie, but I may stand on a desk. I act things out. I dress up in costume. We have fun. You can't assign busy work. They can sniff that out." Ms. Flynn said that students want "a teacher who is fun so that the students enjoy coming to your classroom." Ms. Manning claimed students want "learning to be fun" and that she has "been told many times by students that my class is fun." Ms. Murray referred to the importance of creating a fun learning environment from the student's perspective. She explained:

2

Be goofy, fun, be human. When I make mistakes, I let them know it's okay to correct me. When I was young, you never corrected the teacher. I let them know that I make mistakes too. I'm fun. I love science and math. All of my lessons are hands-on or connected to the real world.

Possessing a high level of teacher energy and enthusiasm.

Many teachers mentioned the significance of possessing and exhibiting a high level of energy and enthusiasm both in and outside the classroom in terms of planning and arranging for meaningful activities. Ms. Miller stated, "I'm enthusiastic, energetic and willing to find out what I'm doing wrong, willing to do the research, long hours, whatever I need to do to reach my students. I put a lot of time and effort into it." Ms. David claimed that characteristics of a highly effective teacher include, "a lot of energy, motivation, and a good rapport with students." Ms. Manning described a highly effective teacher as one who has "a lot of energy." Regarding what she thought students wanted, she stated, "They want to see energy and a positive attitude."

Exhibiting high expectations.

The theme of exhibiting high expectations was a finding. Ms. O'Brien credited her experiences as a military wife and teacher on a military installation for her flexibility, organizational skills, and high expectations of herself and her students. Ms. Lane described herself as having "high expectations for my students and myself."

Ms. Logan advised, "If you don't have high expectations for yourself, you can't expect your students to rise to the top either." Ms. Logan expounded, "If I can keep my expectations high for myself then it's going to positively affect the people around me." Ms. Flynn emphasized the importance of "having high expectations of yourself and your students." Ms. Flynn credited "high expectations from my principal" as a key factor towards her highly effective rating. Ms. Manning offered, "My former principal set higher expectations for me." When asked how she thought her students would define a highly effective teacher, Ms. Murray offered, "A teacher who is a pusher with high expectations and communicates those expectations to the students."

Emphasizing high order thinking skills.

Another finding of highly effective teaching was that of emphasizing higher order thinking skills. For example, Ms. O'Brien claimed that her administrators "stressed higher order thinking questions a lot." Ms. Miller indicated that she made "sure to include higher order thinking questions when lesson planning." When describing her style of teaching, Ms. Lane claimed, "There's a lot of higher order thinking in my classroom. It's important for them to understand the content rather than memorize it." She added, "I see a big shift towards higher order thinking." Ms. Lane referred to workshops on higher order thinking with Bloom's Taxonomy as being the most helpful of all the professional development opportunities in which she's participated. Ms. Logan summarized her questioning philosophy by declaring, "I ask a lot of open ended, higher order questions, and allow students to feed off of those conversations." Ms. David claimed to "enhance" her lesson plans "with HOT [higher order thinking] questions, group activity, hands on, etc."

Maintaining an organized classroom with consistent, structured, student-led routines.

Another finding that defined a highly effective teacher was that of maintaining an organized classroom with consistent, structured, student-led routines.

For example, Ms. Miller defined a highly effective teacher as one who was "always there, always being prepared, being on time, and being organized." She advised, "When they're not engaged and when you're not organized and don't' have management techniques in place, that's when you'll have problems." Among an array of characteristics Ms. Turner claimed her students would describe her as, "organized." Ms. O'Brien listed "organization and being prepared every day" as one of the examples of highly effective teaching in her classroom. Ms. O'Brien pointed to her lesson plan and replied, "I'm an organized person and I have everything that I do on here by topic and date." When Ms. Manning was asked to describe examples of highly effective teaching in other classrooms, she said:

> I see a lot of great classroom management. When I say management, it doesn't necessarily mean discipline; it

means the structure of the classroom in which kids take charge. They know what to do. They've been trained and it's been well organized.

Ms. Manning further commented, "My main focus is engagement with organization and structure coming from my part. She added, "My class was structured so that it was completely student centered in which they had control. They liked it. They felt more accountable. It took pressure off of me. My kids were probably more tired than I was at the end of our class." Ms. O'Brien explained her classroom management routines, "There is structure and the kids know exactly what to do. Structure is what's important at this age level."

When discussing her classroom management procedures, Ms. Franklin stated, "From the very beginning, the first day, our routines go into effect." She emphasized the importance of a structured, yet student-led environment in which students take responsibility for key classroom procedures. She pointed out, "They like structure." Ms. Franklin defined highly effective teaching as being "student-centered." and emphasized the importance of planning for, and facilitating "student-led activities in which the students have responsibilities."

Exhibiting genuine caring, compassionate, empathetic and fair concern for students.

Almost every teacher made reference to the significance of being genuinely caring and having a positive rapport with students which supported this characteristic as a finding descriptive of highly effective teachers. Ms. O'Brien stressed the importance of caring. She said, "I'm old enough to be their grandparent but I try to somehow bond with them. They know I care about them. They know I'm on their side even if I'm angry with them." She further stated, "One kid told me 'you're always happy to be here', so I think it goes back to those same things that I think are most important...caring and being empathetic."

Ms. Miller claimed that many of her students would say, "They love me or I know that she cares about me or I'm consistent and fair." Ms. Franklin said that her students would describe her as "a teacher who cares for them and their learning." Ms. Flynn emphasized the importance of caring as "one of the top characteristics." When Ms. Flynn was asked what she thought might be the definition of a highly effective teacher from a student's perspective, she replied:

> A teacher who never gives up on them who has a loving and caring attitude towards them so that they know that he or she truly cares if they're successful. Most of all, one who is caring...they can sense that.

Ms. Manning listed "caring and compassion for kids" when describing her characteristics as a highly effective teacher. She elaborated, "I think that kids are willing to work for me because they like me and can tell that I like them and am here for them." Ms. Murray claimed she "was raised in a high poverty community, similar to that of her students, and therefore she understands the challenges her students face at home." She expounded:

> A lot of these children don't have love and compassion at home, so I make sure that every morning, no matter what's going on, I meet them at my door with a smile on my face and a hug. They all have my cell phone number so if they had any issues the night before, they can call me. I'll help them with their homework so they know that there's someone who cares about them and their success at school. Children know and can tell that you care.

Ms. Lane credited her personal experiences as a mother of a child with a severe learning disability for the patience, compassion, and desire needed to help all children reach their academic potential. She commented that her students would describe her as "someone who is funny but strict." Additionally, she claimed her students would say that she is "fair."

Ms. O'Brien commented that highly effective teachers "have an ability to be empathetic to their students." She stated that it is wrong to eat or drink in front of students, "not because they're not allowed to eat in class but because we have kids here who may be hungry. How tortuous is it to sit and watch someone eat when you're hungry?"

Ms. Turner cited childhood struggles with dyslexia and an early death of her father as challenges that have strengthened her ability to empathize with at-risk students. Ms. Miller explained that her students would probably mention that she is "consistent, every student would receive the same consequences regardless of who they are." She further explained:

> You have to be fair and consistent with discipline. If the kids know that you love them and are there for them and you're going to be consistent and fair, they'll do what they're supposed to do because you set the bar and they'll meet it.

Ms. Turner recommended that a highly effective teacher "must have passion and compassion." She explained, "You have to have passion for what you teach and compassion for the kids."

2 WHAT CHARACTERISTICS AND KNOWLEDGE CONTRIBUTE TO HIGHLY EFFECTIVE TEACHING?

Participants shared the factors and events that led to highly effective teaching. Findings are reported as emergent themes which included pre-teaching, non-education life experiences, gaining a deeper knowledge of subject content, mentors who provided guidance and inspiration, and personal reflection.

Pre-teaching, non-education life experiences.

Half of the teachers expressed that their pre-teaching careers and experiences were instrumental in their path towards a highly effective teacher rating. Ms. O'Brien credited her experiences as a military wife and teacher on a military installation for her flexibility, organizational skills, and high expectations of herself and her students. She drew from her previous careers as an English teacher in Japan, custom boat builder salesperson, and minor league baseball team representative, among others, to connect her lessons to real world applications. She reflected on her life experiences and declared, "My life experiences have made me a highly effective teacher, not formal education."

Ms. Lane credited her personal experiences as a mother of a child with a severe learning disability for the patience, compassion, and desire needed to help all children reach their academic potential. Ms. Logan quit teaching after her first year and started a new career in a different industry. However, she claimed it was not as fulfilling as teaching and eventually "got back into education." Upon reflecting on that experience between her teaching years, she remarked, "I think that's a major reason for my striving toward highly effectiveness."

Ms. Turner credited her experiences in a non-education workforce and being a military wife for her work ethic and flexibility. When speaking about her pre-teacher experiences, she noted that because she started teaching at a later age than the average teacher, she hasn't "burned out." She commented, "I began teaching at an older age. I was 31 when I began. I was in the workforce where I developed a work ethic."

When asked about significant events that have contributed to her teaching success, Ms. Murray referred to her previous non-education career. She stated, "My financial background has helped. It [previous career] helps me to connect with the real world when I come into my classroom."

Gaining a deeper knowledge of subject content and teaching strategies.

A characteristic that contributed to highly effective teaching was found to be that of gaining a deeper knowledge of subject content and teaching. Most teachers referred to the importance of becoming as knowledgeable as possible on their respective subject content. They mentioned voluntarily attending professional development workshops, conferences, etc. as well as independent research to sharpen or enhance instructional and organizational strategies Ms. O'Brien mentioned subject matter knowledge as an example of highly effective teaching. Ms. Miller defined a highly effective teacher as one who "has knowledge of the concepts, and a deep understanding of the standards." She expanded on her definition by adding, "Knowing from past experiences as a teacher, my strength and weaknesses, and getting into best practices and finding out what is going to reach my students in order to get them the skills they need."

Ms. Lane claimed, "You must have a willingness to go above and beyond...knowledge of the subject content. Ms. Lane pointed out that in order to become a highly effective teacher, one must possess, "a deeper knowledge of the curriculum more so than ever." Ms. Lane exclaimed, "I've always had a sense or knowledge of the curriculum. I've always taught for understanding, not simply just getting through the lesson."

Ms. Franklin defined highly effective teaching as being "student-centered, well-rounded, and knowledgeable of subject content." When asked how her students may describe her, Ms. Turner stated, "A teacher who is organized, knowledgeable of content, nice, helpful, and understanding." Ms. Turner has taken several educational trips, most with students, to various American history-laden locations. She cited those trips as significant experiences in her quest to become "even more knowledgeable" of her course content.

Ms. O'Brien claimed that of all of the professional development opportunities in which she has participated, Kagan strategies and Literacy Design Collaborative (LDC) have been the most beneficial in terms of preparing her for highly effective teaching. She acknowledged:

> The Kagan strategies, as much as I don't like grouping, you don't have to put them in groups to do some of those things. We have workshops and lots of training in Kagan and I think it has helped with higher order questioning techniques. I have also learned a lot by being a part of LDC, even though I don't feel like I can do it to the extent that they would like me to.

Because of her role as a teacher leader, Ms. Franklin was able to frequently observe other highly effective teachers. She noted, "We're doing a lot of Kagan here which is really getting them into cooperative learning and more discussion." Ms. Logan recalled several different professional development opportunities in which she has participated that have led to her highly effective rating. She cited Kagan training as well as a workshop in which the

Common Core State Standards were "unpacked." Regarding the standards unpacking workshop, she noted, "It helped to identify what the actual standard means and how to take the verbs from it and work backwards from there."

Ms. Miller claimed that of all the professional development opportunities in which she has participated, Montessori trainings were "without a doubt, the best." She also went through the Louisiana Teacher Assistance and Assessment Program (LATAAP) mentor training. She described her LATAAP training as one that "made it clear about what the state department identified as effective teaching." Ms. Franklin claimed that of all of the professional development opportunities in which she has participated, "The most beneficial is just collaboration between all of us teachers." She declared, "Everyone has really good ideas. It's just making the time, which is hard during the day. Taking the time to talk and share is important. I talk with teachers across the hall to see how they're teaching different lessons."

When asked about factors that have contributed most to her development as a highly effective teacher, Ms. Flynn credited, "Professional developments workshops, Pinterest [social network sharing website], my coworkers, and high expectations from my principal." She continued, "I'm constantly looking on the internet doing personal research. A lot of highly effective teachers probably post a lot on Pinterest. I don't post much, but I sure do steal from them."

Mentors who provided guidance and inspiration.

Another characteristic and knowledge source that contributed to highly effective teaching was found to be mentors. All participants mentioned having a mentor in their lives who provided guidance and inspiration as well assistance in becoming more proficient in one or more instructional areas. When asked about individuals who have contributed to her becoming a highly effective teacher, Ms. Miller recalled a former colleague from the Montessori school. She explained that at that particular school, there were no doors or permanent walls. She elaborated:

> The lady that taught next to me had much more experience and was a master teacher. She took me under her wing and we opened up that curtain. I was able to see how she modeled lessons with her students, how she used those Montessori materials as well as how she planned lessons. We planned everything together. Being able to have someone like her helped because she modeled classroom management, how to use the materials, how to plan lessons, how to run a classroom where everyone is doing something different and it's not just teacher centered. She was the greatest influence.

When Ms. Turner spoke about her pre-teacher experiences, she noted:

> I've had very good mentors. When I was a student teacher, the lady I student taught under taught me a lot. She was a

nurturer but wasn't one of those sugary kind. You knew she loved you but was strict and I liked that.

When asked which individual(s) contributed to her development as a highly effective teacher, Ms. Manning offered, "Probably number one is my former principal." She emphatically stated, "She was my inspiration as a leader and as a friend." She elaborated:

> She allowed me to be myself, but yet still kind of kept that push. She set higher expectations for me and noticed that I'm not one to fail so she gave me good suggestions in a positive way and again, she had a belief in me because she gave me all these opportunities. She knew I was the type of person who would take advantage of the opportunities and use them to me and my student's advantage. I like that she has a backbone. We didn't always agree on every theory, but yet I like the fact that she stood strongly in what she believed in, but was the first to admit she was wrong if it didn't come out like she expected. I really respect that in a leader.

Ms. Manning also spoke about her father as an inspiration to enter the teaching profession. She expressed:

> As a child, I watched my father as a teacher. He was a huge inspiration. Hearing his students talk about him made me want that same thing. Maybe that was a part of me becoming a teacher. I wanted that affirmation and a part of

something that he was such a huge part of. He made social studies fun because of his passion for history.

When asked about which individuals have contributed to her development as a highly effective teacher, Ms. Logan immediately responded with the name of a current teaching colleague. She explained:

> We were in this together. She came to me for advice and I didn't know what to do and didn't have anything for her other than to help her in teaching writing, because it's an innate thing for me. She was the one that said, "Hey, I read this book. Why don't you read this book?" So she inspired me to read those books and we started talking about the books. We'd ask each other, "Did you try this, or that?"

Ms. Logan recalled that she has "taught with a lot of people through the years because I've bounced around a lot and I think I've learned something from every single teacher, but one that stands out was an old school teacher." She shared about that early experience:

> She taught me how to read test scores and to work from student strengths and weaknesses and how to work towards improving by meeting them where they were. Before the value-added model, when I first started, it [school performance score] was about how many students scored proficient. Before VAM [value-added model], I already worked under the understanding that I have to get every kid

to grow academically. I think it was my old teacher friend who helped me to see how to do that.

Personal reflection.

Several teachers emphasized the importance of reflecting on the success or failures of procedures and methods as a characteristic and source of knowledge that contributed to highly effective teaching. They talked about internally processing how their instructional approaches and student assessments could be better. Ms. Logan defined highly effective teaching as, "a vocation, a calling." She said with passion and conviction, "It starts with the self. Your personal being. I see teaching as a call of duty, not as a job." She described effective teachers as those who "constantly reflect on practices in the classroom and try to identify weaknesses and strengths and figure out what to do to get better." She added, "I've always been a reflective person, thinking there's got to be a better way." Ms. Logan expounded, "The proactive approach to self-study and professional development is key."

Ms. Franklin stated, "When the rubric came out, I reflected on what I was already doing versus what I needed to do and thought about what I needed to do to get there. It wasn't so overwhelming. We were already doing it; we just needed to take it a step further." Regarding student assessment results, Ms. Franklin offered, "Sometimes I allow them to retake tests based on when the majority of the class struggles, which means they weren't ready. I then reflect on what I did or didn't do and then we come back and do it a different way and hopefully the second way is more effective." When discussing the post observation conference, she noted, "It really makes you reflect on how to improve what you're doing to get better."

Ms. Lane cited her experience of earning a national board certification. She recalled:

> When I went through the [teacher national board] certification process, it makes you look at yourself from every angle. It was a tough experience but it forces you to analyze yourself as a teacher and makes you aware of every aspect of teaching because of the way it's designed.

3 WHAT PRACTICES CONTRIBUTE TO HIGHLY EFFECTIVE TEACHING?

The participants shared the practices and methods of highly effective teaching. Based on their comments, findings, reported as emergent themes, included lesson planning strategies, meaningful activities, questioning and discussion techniques, classroom management routines, expectations and procedures, assessment of content mastery with remediation opportunities.

Lesson planning strategies.

Lesson planning strategies were identified as contributing to highly effective teaching. Most teachers described their lesson planning strategy as a process that involved referring to the course standards, taking into account available resources, using pre-assessments to determine baseline data, and the incorporation of meaningful, high order thinking activities. When asked about preparing high quality and rigorous lesson plans in terms of setting instructional outcomes, Ms. Miller replied:

First, I go through what it is that I want to teach. I go
through the GLEs [Grade Level Expectations] and decide
what I need to teach for the year. Then, I go through
whatever resources I have in hand. I go through the
textbook, pull resources from the internet and other books I
have in the classroom. Then, I start looking at the
observation rubric. I know what I need to do. I must have
an objective on the wall and state it so the kids understand
it. I look at that rubric as I'm planning out the lesson to be
sure that I hit all of the things that I need to have in there. I
make sure to include higher order thinking questions and
technology when lesson planning. So, I start with the
GLEs [Grade Level Expectations] and then I find resources
and then as I begin to build the lesson plan, I focus on the
rubric and think of the best teaching practices to use.

When asked about preparing high quality and rigorous lesson
plans in terms of setting instructional outcomes, Ms. Lane
emphasized the importance of being very familiar with the subject
standards and explained:

The first thing I do is unpack the standards. You have to be
very familiar with the standards. Then, I determine how
I'm going to approach it, and put it in sequential order.
Then, I prepare my lessons. We don't have a lot of
resources. I make my own plans. There are a few things I
can find but I'm not by the book at all. They're more in my
head than anything. I'm not real formal with lesson plans.

It's usually in a notebook or on a piece of paper. I could write one that is formal but I wouldn't even look at it. I know what I need to do. I know what I have to teach. I just kind of go with it. Whatever the concept is, I want them to fully understand it. For observations, I write a picture perfect one. I can make it look nice and neat.

When asked about preparing high quality and rigorous lesson plans in terms of setting instructional outcomes, Ms. Franklin replied, "I work backwards. I look at my assessments, and especially test items that are released by the state." She described her planning process:

Being a teacher in a high stakes testing year, I think about which skills have not been taught yet to get us where we need to be. The lesson activities are designed with students being able to think for themselves. Then, I'll look back at the standard to make sure everything is aligned. I can't plan too far in advance. Lesson plans are due on Monday so I put them together on Thursday and Friday although I come up on Sundays a lot to finalize them. It probably takes me about an hour to an hour and a half to plan for the week.

Ms. Logan claimed lesson planning has not been her strongest virtue in the past. However, she discussed using new strategies when she returns to the classroom next semester:

I am taking a class on that [lesson planning] right now. The book is called, *Integrating Differentiated Instruction*

and Understanding by Design by Tomli
It teaches how to start from the big pictu
standard and then you work backwards
worked backwards from the LEAP test
know what else to do. I know that's not a good thing, but
what else was I going to do? I didn't know! In the future, I
will utilize backwards planning from common core
standards and establish targeted goals and student friendly
objectives. Then, I will generate several essential or guided
questions as a map towards the outcome. I also want to
integrate with my co-teachers to make sure that we have a
cohesive unit.

When asked about preparing high quality and rigorous lesson
plans in terms of setting instructional outcomes, Ms. Turner
explained, "I print the test out first. That way, it keeps me on
track. From there, I have a whole unit where it's everything they
need to know. It's backwards design."

When asked about preparing high quality and rigorous lesson
plans setting instructional outcomes, Ms. David replied,
"Whenever I know I'm going to be observed, I spend weeks
designing a lesson whereas truth be known, I don't do that on a
daily basis." She added, "It makes me sound brilliant, but I'm not,
I'm just a regular teacher." She continued:

I'll try to find something online that's been vetted that goes
along with my textbook because we weren't' given anything
other than websites to look at. Until I get a new textbook,

I've decided I'm going to use mine, add to it, and enhance it with HOT [higher order thinking] questions, group activity, hands on, etc.

The textbook has definitely been a help this year to get us through what was supposed to be a transitional year. I make sure I include everything. I do warm up, teacher activity, student activity; list all math practices, accelerated math [software program]. I plan formally about a week in advance, but I have the course informally planned out to the end of the year on the calendar. It's not fancy. I know exactly what we're going to do up until the last day of school.

When asked about preparing high quality and rigorous lesson plans in terms of setting instructional outcomes, Ms. Flynn replied, "I like to do that backwards in which you make the test first by looking at the standards, what the students need to know, and then teach them to be successful in meeting those standards." She expounded:

We're following Engage New York [curriculum]. I like it because of the way the lessons are designed. They start off very hands on, very visual; and then they move to paper and pencil. The first questions are, "Here's the problem. Work it," and then it moves into word problems where the last word problem is very high level. I start with the end in mind. What is my test going to look like? What do my students need to know based on the standards and how will I teach them to be successful on the test?

Ms. Manning referred to her "theory on highly effective teaching" when asked about preparing high quality and rigorous lesson plans. She expounded on her theory and explained in detail her planning process:

> My lesson plans revolve around my students being the leaders of my classroom. I plan my lessons where it's very little whole group in favor of small grouping. However, it has to be thought out because your lessons and activities have to be constructed where students can take charge and yet have some [teacher] leadership in there with questioning prompts. I train my students on the questioning techniques through my own modeling and I have questioning cards to help with things like that. By the end of the year, they didn't need those questioning prompts.
>
> My main focus is engagement with organization and structure coming from my part. In the perfect world, I developed the unit first. I did pretesting because I did differentiated instruction. Therefore, I needed the pretest to tell me what my groups were. Teaching math, you can't formulate your groups from the beginning of the year testing. I may have had someone who was great at algebra, but when it came to geometry needed to change groups. Pretesting was a huge part of lesson planning. After the pretest, I based my timeline on what was needed. I usually

referenced ten to twenty minutes per day for whole group, a daily instruction to introduce the overall concept, and then we broke out into sessions. I unit planned, but my unit plans with the weekly plans changed often depending on what the week's outcomes looked like.

Ms. Murray described the following procedure regarding preparing high quality and rigorous lesson plans in terms of setting instructional outcomes:

First, go to the standards. They drive the instruction. I always start with my assessment piece first. From my assessment and tasks, that's how I plan my lesson so I'll know how high to hit. It's very important to start with those standards first, but not just with your grade level standards because if they master those, you've got to be ready to dive into the next grade level standards.

Meaningful activities.

Every teacher emphasized the significance of incorporating meaningful, high order thinking activities in their daily lessons as a practice that contributed to highly effective teaching. Most implied that keeping students engaged in meaningful and interesting activities led to a classroom in which discipline issues were minimal or even non-existent. Ms. Flynn commented, "I use a lot of hands on, visual activities." Ms. Miller expressed, "I try to gear my hands on activities to have a HOT [high order thinking] part to them where they're having to create something or evaluate or analyze something or compare and contrast. Ms. Miller emphasized, "The key is in keeping students' attention by incorporating a variety of interesting and fun activities in her lessons with seamless transitions."

Ms. Franklin said that her students would describe her as "a teacher who takes the time to plan activities that they're interested in." She added, "The lesson activities are designed with students being able to think for themselves." When asked to elaborate on the activities, Ms. Franklin offered, "The activities are relevant to them. For example, I incorporate video games they're interested in. They actually designed one of the centers during an activity on area and perimeter." She emphasized that students "create their own questions." With a sense of pride and accomplishment, she added, "As each team rotates to each center, they're answering the questions generated by their classmates."

Questioning and discussion techniques.

Questioning and discussion techniques were found to contribute to highly effective teaching. All teachers pointed out the value of having an effective questioning and discussion set of strategies in place in order to facilitate an atmosphere conducive to critical thinking. When asked to elaborate on her questioning methods, Ms. Miller offered:

> I write two or three questions while I'm lesson planning.
> Sometimes during the course of the class, I'll think of
> something else that may be a good question based on

something a student says or asks. We have a question and discussion time during class in which they try to build their skills of meaningful discussion. It is a hard skill to learn in 5th grade because they don't want to discuss with me much less than with each other. They're scared of saying something wrong. They don't want to say, "Well, I think something different." Nobody wants to be wrong so we have to work through those skills of how to have a meaningful discussion.

I try to gear my hands on activities to have a HOT part to them where they're having to create something or evaluate or analyze something or compare and contrast. With the new observation rubric, you have to do a lot of discussion. A lot of that tends to be teacher guided because kids aren't ready yet to discuss. In middle school and high school, they have their own thoughts and know how to communicate them but at the elementary level, they're not ready for that. They look to you to see if it's the right answer. They won't say anything else until you validate their answer. I have to use techniques to turn it so that it becomes more child-centered.

Ms. Lane claimed that orchestrating high-level questioning and discussion is an important aspect of guiding her students to being critical thinkers and not just memorizers. She described:

At the beginning of the year, I actually show them Bloom's Taxonomy at a kid level. They see the difference between

LOT [lower order thinking] and HOT [higher order thinking]. So, they understand that in a discussion, we don't just call out things; we want to have a meaningful discussion. We do an activity called stop/swap, turn/talk. We do it at the beginning and they actually have to write about what we discussed in their journal. After they finish writing, they swap. They can't be critical, they can criticize, but not in a mean way. They just have to point out what was good or what was misunderstood and then they turn and talk about it. From there, whatever lends itself to a discussion, we go with. Sometimes I have to intervene because they'll want to talk for the whole class period. Sometimes it's like pulling teeth, other times it's easy. But it's spontaneous more than anything.

Ms. Franklin claimed that high-level questioning and discussion are a common occurrence in her classroom. However, she stressed that it requires time, practice and patience to orchestrate. She explained:

It's a lot of modeling at first. If a student notices that his or her partner is struggling, we don't want to see them struggle so they start asking questions such as, "What do you think about doing it a different way, can we think of it differently?" It's teaching them to think differently. In fourth grade, I would say by late November, they're able to ask those questions and start thinking on that higher level. They practice and get better throughout the year. When I can actually cut back on the modeling and say, "What do I expect to hear?" They'll say, "Good questions. Good discussions."

Ms. Logan noted that orchestrating high-level questioning and discussion is an area in which she uses "a lot of partner talks." She prefers groups of two students rather than four "because they have more turns to participate." She credited scaffolding as a means of meeting students where they are and progressively moving them toward stronger understanding and greater independence in the learning process.

Ms. David claimed that orchestrating high-level questioning and discussion is an area in which she encourages a student-led process. She invests time at the beginning of the school year modeling meaningful questioning with expectations that her students will eventually lead that process. After a student leads the questioning and discussion activity, they'll review and critique the session. She noted, "It's positive. We don't criticize."

Ms. Manning claimed that she used Bloom's Taxonomy when developing lesson plans in order to orchestrate high-level questioning and discussion. She explained:

> I always utilize through Blooms [Taxonomy], questioning prompts that would not just help me, but would help the students question each other. I modeled and then had questioning prompts which I called talking cards at the tables all the time. When the students got a little lost when talking with each other, they could flip through the cards to

help move the discussion along. This was every day, all day. Questioning was a huge part of my classroom. I use the talking cards, not because I needed them but for modeling for them. Through modeling, we did open versus close ended questions just to see the difference between the two.

Orchestrating high-level questioning and discussion is a strategy in which Ms. Murray used "a lot of different resources" including ideas she finds on Pinterest [social network sharing website]. She used "a Kagan questioning card" as well as "a flip chart with Bloom's taxonomy to help me development my questions." She expounded:

> I let the students ask the questions. I plan for questioning to make sure that I hit all the points. Accountable talk anchors are on a poster for reference. They're used to answering, not asking questions, so the poster helps to initialize their questions. When they answer, they can't just say "yes or no." They have to continue by saying, "because" and then refer to a text-based source to support their answer. After they refer to the text, then they can refer to a personal experience.

Classroom management routines, expectations and procedures.
Another finding was the important contribution of classroom management routines, expectations, and procedures to highly effective teaching. When I asked Ms. O'Brien to describe her daily

31

classroom routine, she started by talking about a daily assignment in which important historical events of that date are reviewed:

> I try to make it relevant to what we're studying that day but the calendar doesn't always cooperate. Some days, it's just a cultural thing I think they ought to know about. Some of these kids have never heard an Elvis or Sinatra song or have seen or know who Buddy Holly is. It's cultural stuff. But every day they come in and copy that and once a month we go through them and I give them a little quiz and it's just a matter of what happened on this day just to make sure they're doing it. That's their first job every day. They know where to pick stuff up and then we start the lesson. I always try to lead-in that way and then we go through the material. That's why procedure every day is important.
>
> I use a lot of music and video of the time when and where it's applicable. Finally, the powers that be last year gave us the freedom to use YouTube. A lot of times, that's how I end a lesson. I try to incorporate music. I find that's a really good way to get their attention and it helps them learn things. But every day starts with structure, with the same process every day."

When asked about her classroom routines and procedures, Ms. Miller said that every student has a job and they know what is expected. She takes pride in saying that her classroom runs with very little guidance. She explained:

> I try to run my classroom so that it runs without me being

there. I believe that classroom management is not just making them behave. It's about a set of procedures that you have in your classroom. Students like consistency and routine. At the beginning of the school year, we go through the whole PBIS set of rules at school and talk about what they look like. We write our own rules and discuss the expectations. I set up a lot of routines such as how to sharpen their pencil, go to the restroom, and get tissue. Then we talk about how to handle materials in the science lab and the jobs that each student has.

Being respectful and all of those things line up for the rest of the year and I have to be consistent for it to run smoothly. They know there are consequences for negative behavior. I have very little disrespect because they know I respect them. I don't yell and scream because I don't think that's needed. They know when I'm upset without having to raise my voice. We set up transitions like how to line up in the hallway, get books out, and get ready for the next activity. We're constantly moving, discussing, taking notes, conducting a hands-on activity or watching a video clip. I know that if I don't' keep them engaged, that's when we have behavior problems. They're focused on science and aren't thinking about how they can misbehave.

When we discussed her classroom management philosophy, Ms. Lane noted that she invests time at the beginning of the school year talking with her students about the importance of gaining a quality education. She commented:

> They learn at the beginning of the school year. We sit
> down and talk about why we're here. They get a behavior
> chart that eventually fades out because it's not needed after
> a few weeks because they get used to the routine. I don't
> have a lot of discipline problems. I tell them what I expect.
> If they don't do what they're supposed to do, there are
> consequences, if they do what they're supposed to do, they
> get privileges.

When discussing her classroom management procedures, Ms. Franklin stated, "From the very beginning, the first day, our routines go into effect." She emphasized the importance of a structured, yet student-led environment in which students take responsibility for key classroom procedures. When asked to describe her classroom management structure, Ms. Logan claimed that she was not a "natural born disciplinarian," but doesn't have significant discipline issues in her classroom. She has instituted a "democratic environment" in order to "teach students how to work cooperatively." She emphasized, "They need to be taught self-discipline."

When discussing her classroom management procedures and routines, Ms. Turner mentioned the significance of taking advantage of every instructional minute from bell to bell. She noted:

> When they walk in, they know exactly what's going to take
> place. I have the page on the board, what they need to turn

in, and a reminder to sharpen your pencil. We walk in as a
class, so they know to take care of things quickly before we
get going. Sometimes I assign jobs to students, such as to
tell students what they need to do when they're absent.
Sometimes I'll do a warm-up, but to me bell ringers take up
too much instructional time unless we're reviewing for the
iLEAP.   It's expectations; they know what's going to
happen. Daily routines, same thing happens every day.
My classroom may be rearranged, but I never have my
desks in rows. They're always facing different ways,
because I like to have the stage. By this time, the kids
know what to do and will redirect each other. At the end of
the class, we recap the day's lesson.

When Ms. David discussed her routines and procedures
regarding classroom management, she reiterated her emphasis on
maximizing instructional classroom time. She elucidated:

They have warm up right when they come in the door. I
give them about five minutes and right now it's consisting
of the new iLEAP practice test assessment items a page a
day, about three questions on the page. Then, I choose a
random student. They love to go to the board and play
teacher. They facilitate the discussion of the questions.
They don't just go up there and solve it, they have to use
HOT [higher order thinking] questions and get that
discussion going. Then, we talk about our purpose
statement of what we're going to do today. Afterwards, we

go into the lesson. I facilitate the notes.

I think it's important that they do see an example of modeling first. I go over a new assignment or new lesson and then after about 25-30 minutes of discussing and practicing it, they're given an assignment. Sometimes its independent work designed to last about 15 minutes. Sometimes its group work. If it's independent, we always have a partner check the next day. After the lesson, they start their independent mode. Even if its group work, they go into their accelerated math [software program]. It's all individualized.

When I asked Ms. Flynn to describe her daily classroom routine, she confidently stated, "When they come in, they know to unpack, get out their homework from the night before, and there's always a bell ringer on the board. They know exactly what to do." Ms. Flynn protects instructional time by using signals or gestures to nonverbally communicate with students and checks homework while students are working on the bell-ringer.

When I asked Ms. Manning to describe her daily classroom routines and procedures, she emphasized the importance of continuous engagement and her role as a facilitator. She reasoned and elucidated:

From the minute they walk in, besides the greeting I give them, it's important to begin with engagement. I knew if I didn't have a task waiting for them, it would take five to ten minutes to get them on task when I was ready. Something right then and there as soon as they walk in is key. After they did a daily activity, then we would begin the whole group type of discussion. Even though I was teaching in front of the class, I was always engaging my students with questioning, getting feedback from them. Often times, students would take over that whole group part and then break into small group stations during which I would pull students in small groups to give them what they needed based on that pretest.

In my classroom, I was more of a facilitator. My students took charge from the time they walked in. I had a job for every student. I never picked up technology or other resource and materials. The jobs change. You know there's certain jobs for certain students based on their uniqueness. My class was structured so that it was completely student centered in which they had control. They liked it. They felt more accountable. It took pressure off of me. My kids were probably more tired than I was at the end of our class.

When I asked Ms. Murray to describe her classroom routines and procedures, she started by mentioning that she's "never had an issue with discipline." She claimed, "My principal wonders why we never send kids to the office." Ms. Murray then proceeded to share her methods of dealing with those rare occasions when students did not meet classroom expectations. She explained that she doesn't have classroom rules; instead she has a "discipline cycle." She displayed a small stack of laminated cards and said:

If a student gets off task or is doing something like talking during instruction, the "1" card goes on their desk. That's a nonverbal warning to get on task. After a while, if they got back on task with no further issues, I'd pick it up and place a different card on their desk which thanked them for positive behavior. If they didn't get back on task, I'd flip the one to a two, get in their ear and tell them, "If you continue to disrupt the class, then you're going to choose from the negative consequences menu." It wasn't my choice. It was their choice. That removes the teacher from the negative consequence process and makes it less personal.

They also fill out a reflection form that goes in their folder and a copy goes home to the parents. That process kept them out of the office. By giving them that choice, it was like being a little adult in the classroom. So simple. Yet so effective. That's modeling how important it is to not distract the class.

Assessment of content mastery with remediation opportunities.

Another finding regarding practices that contribute to highly effective teaching was that of assessment of content mastery with remediation opportunities. All teachers explained their assessment process as one in which content mastery is the primary focus. Half of the teachers also mentioned the importance of pre-assessments to gather baseline data, providing immediate feedback and opportunities for remediation to correct wrong answers or mistakes. Ms. O'Brien took pride in stating that no student has failed her class for the past two years. In fact, she said, "I tell them at the beginning of the year that it's as hard to fail my class as it is to make an A. I help them a lot, they can come in here during lunch and they can help each other."

In a discussion regarding assessment and monitoring of student learning, Ms. Miller noted that she begins each school year with a science inventory questionnaire of her students during which they "talk about their interests in science." In terms of monitoring student learning, she commented, "I look at their previous year's LEAP scores. I look at their weaknesses and make note of those when we get to that content area." When the topic shifted to assessments, she elaborated:

> We take chapter tests based on the textbook which is based on common core. It covers all the GLEs [Grade Level Expectations], it's awesome. I base my summative assessments on those chapters. If one or more students totally miss a concept, then I need to go back and either pull that one child or teach the whole class for whatever reason and re-teach that concept. In between, during every lesson, I use formative assessments such as thumbs up/down. We write answers on student white boards. I formatively assess their discussion questions, participation, and stations. They have to record everything they do

whether its reading comprehension or they're actually designing an experiment.

A lot of times they don't recognize words seen on state testing; therefore we have to work on vocabulary. We use exit cards at the end of the day to tell me what they learned, didn't learn, they rate themselves. Those things really help me during the course of the lesson because sometimes you have to change your lesson for the next day. If they didn't get it, there's no sense in continuing. With science, as far as standardized test prep, there's very little out there. We spend our time instead focusing on mastering skills. We talk about how to look at a question and process that information, how to cross out, how to draw pictures, how to reason if you don't exactly know the answer. I look at how they scored on the iLEAP to plan for how I'll improve the following year by noting the concepts in which they were weak. From that data, I focus on what I can do better. I chart it each year, making note of the areas in which I need to improve.

In a discussion regarding assessment and monitoring student learning, Ms. Lane expressed concern with district-wide, mandated assessments by saying, "Benchmark math tests are dictated by the district. The tests are generated by a computer program but they don't always go along with the content." In terms of how students are otherwise assessed formally in her classes, she explained:

Tests are broken down into units. I also use self-made

assessments. I do allow students to retake tests sometimes where I'll take an average of the two. Or, sometimes I allow an alternative assessment such as an essay.

Regarding formative assessment, she stated, "I ask a lot of informal questions to see if they're paying attention."

Ms. Franklin explained that her formal assessments are carefully designed and timed. She stressed the importance of assessing her students only after she feels they're ready. She reasoned:

> They're tested so much. I wait until they're ready. I give formal assessments at the end of each standard that I teach. It's not really set. It's when I feel like they're ready. I don't rush a test just because I have to get a grade in. We test when I feel they're ready. My tests include multiple choice, explaining, and written expression. Sometimes I allow them to retake tests based on when the majority of the class struggles, which means they weren't ready. I then reflect on what I did or didn't do and then we come back and do it a different way and hopefully the second way is more effective. However, the need for retesting doesn't happen often.

Regarding assessment, Ms. Logan shared that "conferencing is one of the things that I do now that I didn't realize before was a best practice." She elaborated and provided an example:

> When I teach writing, I didn't know how else to do this but I'd call the kids up one at a time to go over what they

wrote. I would give them corrective feedback. This is how you fix this or that. That's a very effective way. I didn't know that was so effective until hindsight. An example is that a summative assessment wasn't working because all of the years I taught 4th grade, I'd always give them a written response question, one per week, because I feel like quality over quantity is better. It didn't always have to have evidence from the passage, but I did include that when it became a component. What I would get when I first started teaching was a one sentence answer and I wouldn't let them go back and fix it. I now allow them to go back. I'll say, "This is not enough. I need you to tell me more. Can you go back and reread this part?" and only until they meet my standards, can they then turn in the test. I thought I was wrong for that. Like I'm cheating, but now I realize I'm just giving them corrective feedback. They'll never give me what I'm asking them to do if I don't show them.

Ms. Logan concluded our discussion regarding assessment by stating, "I use formative assessment to drive instruction."

In a discussion regarding assessment and monitoring student learning, Ms. Turner started by describing her formative assessment strategies. She commented:

I don't' have activotes [electronic response system], so they fold paper into four sections. I'll ask a question. It'll be multiple choice. They close their eyes before giving me the answer. That's just for me to see if they got it and we can move on. There are different things in the toolbox to see if they get it or not. I use a lot of questioning. If I see they don't have it, I go back and re-teach.

Ms. Turner then proceeded to explain her summative assessment methods with an emphasis on the importance of using a format similar to that of the state standardized test. She described in more detail:

> Each chapter of the book has four sections. With each section, I'll use the reproducible if it's good. I'll have a vocabulary test and then an iLEAP [state standardized test] style test at the end of the unit. I don't want busy work. An iLEAP style test is one in which there are both multiple choice and about four questions to answer but they choose two open-ended or constructed response questions. That way, when they do get to the real iLEAP, they're familiar with the format.
>
> On test day, I'll go over a few things before the test. On the day before, we take the whole class period and study together using jeopardy games and such. They know exactly what's going to be on the test. I don't have any surprises. I'll walk around and when I see they're finishing, I'll go back to my desk. They'll come up to me and I'll glance real quick and mark the ones they got wrong, hand it back to them. They go back to their seats correct it, and turn it in. They're not able to use their notes, but this process gets them to rethink their wrong answer. With

computers, I can now upload my tests so it's read to those students who need the test read aloud to meet their IEP requirements.

In a discussion regarding assessment and monitoring student learning, Ms. David was quick to point out that her students have said that she's "the fastest teacher at getting our grades back to us." She expounded:

> I grade all tests that night. They get it back the next day and talk about it as soon as they come in. I think immediate feedback is very important because they can still remember what they were thinking when they put that answer. If you wait too long, they don't remember why or how they put the wrong answer.

Regarding how she constructs and grades her summative assessments, Ms. David said, "I use some questions from the textbook and I'll use some from the practice iLEAP tests even if it doesn't relate to the topic we're learning at that time." She continued:

> They know that those practice questions can be in there at any time. I'll pull some activities from the internet and ask specific questions from those activities. I try for the tests to not be too lengthy. I feel like they're challenged, but I should say that my average is usually about 90%. I think that's because they get a very similar quiz, a little smaller, maybe 20 questions the day before. We go over it right before the test and then they get a 50 question test. If I had

a lot of kids not do well, we'd have a retest, but that doesn't happen very often at all.

In a discussion regarding assessment and monitoring student learning, Ms. Manning accentuated the importance of measuring growth and content mastery. She explained:

I started pre assessments about five years ago and realized the importance of those because of the small grouping. Through the pre assessments, I knew that small grouping would change throughout the year as different students had different strengths and weaknesses. I informally assess a lot. I do a lot of spot checking, walking around, questioning.

As far as formal assessments, I use Eagle [online assessment instrument] or some other online resource to formulate those tests. Those were done in advance to lesson planning and instruction. My unit assessments were the summative assessments. My pre- and post-tests looked similar if not identical. I needed to know where they were in the pre-test and then measure their growth level on the post test. There is always an opportunity to retest. It's not about grades, it's about understanding. I wanted the grade to reflect their true level of understanding. My students were very clear about having the opportunity to improve; they just needed to work towards that.

Regarding assessment and monitoring student learning, Ms. Murray stated, "I ask a lot of questions and they ask a lot of questions." She initially mentioned an emphasis on self-assessment:

> When they come up to present or explain their work, they also can rate themselves. When they fill out an exit ticket, it'll tell me their level of understanding according to their own perception. They rate themselves.

Ms. Murray then explained her methods and theory of student assessment in terms of content mastery. She illustrated:

> When they go to stations, I use the data I'm able to pull up to determine grades. I have student conferences, just me sitting one on one with a student during their PE time. I work with Coach. It's very organized and it only takes about four minutes per student. We do that every two weeks. It's just an individual check in.

4 WHAT TYPES OF SUPPORT SYYSTEMS CONTRIBUTE TO HIGHLY EFFECTIVE TEACHING?

Participants shared examples of support systems that contributed to highly effective teaching. The interviewees identified three findings which are reported as emergent themes that included effectively communicating with administrators prior to an observation, gaining a clear understanding of the expectations in the observation rubric and receiving and heeding immediate feedback following an observation.

Effectively communicating with administrators.

Effectively communicating with administrators was found to be a support system that contributed to highly effective teaching. For example, when asked about how her administrator(s) prepared her for the classroom observations, Ms. O'Brien replied, "They stressed the higher order thinking questions a lot. They do not want to see teachers sitting behind their desk." She explained the observation process:

> We had walk-throughs and I kind of enjoyed it. They noted if the objective was on the board. When they talked to a kid, they wanted to know if the student knew what the lesson was and why it was being done. That's the type of classroom they're looking for and want to see. They also told us that most of us are doing a good job and there was nothing to be nervous about, keep doing what you're doing and you'll be fine. There wasn't much of a stress level if you knew you were doing the best you could do and therefore you didn't have to worry about the observation. Again, they stressed engagement and higher order thinking questions.

Reflecting on the observation experience, Ms. Miller recalled that last year she met with both the principal and assistant principal and they both conducted the formal observation. She stressed how important it was to meet with them before the observation to discuss or describe unique situations in terms of student needs and behaviors. Ms. Miller sincerely valued the post-observation feedback she received. She explained:

> I was able to tell them about how the kids had jobs and they already know what to do. I was able to tell them about what they're going to see so that during the stations, if they don't make it around to each station, they know what's going on in all the stations.

Ms. Franklin remarked, "I really like the pre-observation conference because it makes you think about your lesson before it happens." When reflecting on the observation experience, Ms. Logan explained:

> I was able to type up exactly what she should look for. They gave us the opportunity to point out something I or the students did that they may not have seen. They allowed us to come in and justify that we did meet a component. Because we were allowed to turn the pre-observation answers in written form, I was able to clearly articulate what the observer(s) would see before the lesson. That way, they could look for those things in particular. I was able to frontload the observer with what I was going to do. In case they missed something while I taught, they would have that to go back on and jog their memory.

Ms. Turner indicated that her administrators helped to put her at ease. She recalled, "They just told me to do what I do best. They tell me what the rubric needs and they explain to me everything that the rubric says, what they have to look for. I love that they took the stress off.

When asked about how her administrator(s) prepared her for the classroom observations, Ms. Flynn replied, "We had a pre-observation conference in which we looked at the lesson plans, the rubric and what she'll be looking for during the observation." She added, "We have that time to talk about some unique situations in terms of students who have special needs or requirements."

Ms. Manning commented, "We had a pre-observation meeting in which we went over the expectations. We went over my lesson plan. We discussed it." She added:

> Both administrators gave me suggestions. They wanted me to elaborate a little more in some areas at times. I think it was great leadership on their part. It wasn't that they disagreed with what I was doing; they just wanted to make sure that I had all of the components adequately addressed.

When reflecting on the observation experience, Ms. Murray said, "With the pre-observation conference, I was able to make my evaluator aware of situations in my room such as students who have unique or special needs." She elaborated, "I'm able to explain to him why I may focus more on one or two students. I'd rather get observed unannounced, but the preconference works because it gives me an opportunity to explain what he'll probably see and why."

Gaining a clear understanding of the expectations in the observation rubric.

Another support system that contributed to highly effective teaching was that of understanding the expectations in the observation rubric. When asked how her administrator(s) prepared her for the classroom observations, Ms. Miller indicated that she had a significant amount of meaningful training, support, and preparation. She explained:

We had several faculty meeting sessions in which they went through the rubric at the beginning of the year so we had time to study it and start planning lessons. They showed us videos of highly effective and ineffective teaching so that we could see what it looks like and what it doesn't look like. They emphasized student choice in the rubric. They made it clear about what they were going to look for and gave us some ideas to use. They gave us opportunities to practice with them about what they were looking for before the actual observations.

Ms. Lane noted that her administrator(s) prepared her for the classroom observations in the following manner, "She called us all in and told us what they would be looking for and gave us the rubric. We talked about the components and what they meant along with examples of what they should look like."

Ms. Franklin explained that her administrator(s) prepared her for the classroom observations by saying:

We were given the rubric before the school year started. We went over the rubric, each part extensively. We were given time to talk with our coworkers within our grade levels and other grade levels about how we would do this.

When asked how her administrator(s) prepared her for the classroom observations, Ms. Logan replied, "They gave us a copy of the observation rubric ahead of time to look at and study. I started using that as a guide to prepare myself for my observation."

Ms. David stated that she was already familiar with the rubric from some of her recent college courses.

Ms. Murray exclaimed, "I actually bought my own book by Danielson to prepare myself." She continued, "I think when the rubric first came out, a lot of people were just guessing at what the rubric meant, so I got that book and studied it." She also noted that she consulted with a teacher friend who taught at a different school who "helped to understand what they'd be looking for."

Receiving and heeding immediate feedback following an observation.

Receiving and heeding immediate feedback following observations was found to be a valuable support that contributed to highly effective teaching. When reflecting on the observation experience, Ms. O'Brien said, "That has changed a lot of the way that I teach to make sure that I do those things. It made me question, am I providing an opportunity for every kid to get it?"

Ms. Miller stated, "After the observation, they gave some ideas on how to improve or do things differently and I like that because no one is perfect. It's great for someone else to give you feedback because no one can think of everything. It's good to have a set of fresh eyes giving you ideas on how to improve. Regarding post observation conferences, she stated, "I really like the feedback because if I'm not doing what I need to be doing to hit all those points, then I need to adjust something." She recalled:

In my first observation, I had one student who was not actively engaged the whole time. Afterwards I took the advice and thought, "How can I get him more involved and give him more responsibility? That's really what he wanted. He wanted that coordinator role. It really makes you reflect on how to improve what you're doing to get better.

Ms. Logan exclaimed, "The post observation conferences were face-to-face and that was beneficial to hear someone else's perspective. I could see where I need to work from and improve. Ms. Turner said, "They make me think...how can I do it better?" She further acknowledged the support she received from her administrators:

Things that I don't see that they see, help me to get better. The principal gave me an idea on how to make sure that all students are actively engaged by just asking the question, "How am I sure that all are involved?" They make me feel good about myself. They're my cheerleaders. Anything they want me to change or do, I'll do because they support me.

Ms. David reflected on the observation and post-observation conference process. She said:

I think it helped me to see where I need to grow. Some of my questions weren't as high order and critical thinking as they needed to be. I realized that was something I had to work on. Being able to talk about it right after was beneficial.

Reflecting on the benefits of the observation experience, Ms. Flynn recalled, "She was able to point some things out that I didn't see." She continued, "While I'm teaching next time, I'll be aware of those things. It was great feedback on what I'm doing right as well as what I need to improve on."

When reflecting on the observation conferences, Ms. Manning said, "It was beneficial because I used that fall observation as an opportunity to change what I needed in the spring to make sure I stayed at the highly effective level. I was able to use their feedback to improve on my spring lesson planning."

Ms. Murray offered, "The post-observation conference gives you that immediate feedback. I don't care how highly effective you are. There's always something I can do a little bit better." She added:

> What I like about our evaluators, he told me, "What I saw was this, but if you did this one thing, it would bring you from here to here." He takes the time to go through it. He even records it on his iPad so he's able to point out, "If you would have done this..." If you stop growing, something's wrong. You get that refinement and you know where to go from there. Don't just tell me this is my issue and not offer a solution.

5. MS. O'BRIEN

Ms. O'Brien has been in education for 20 years with the 10 most recent as a classroom teacher. She currently teaches 7th grade American History and two classes of 8th grade Introduction to Business Computer Applications (IBCA). She previously taught adult education, French, typing and English. She obtained her bachelor's degree from a regional university in north Louisiana. She is certified to teach Social Studies, English, Adult Ed. and Business Ed. The school at which she taught during the 2013-2014 school year is located in an urban area where 49% of the student population qualified for free or reduced lunch. She brings to the classroom a variety of life experiences that greatly enhance her social studies lessons. She draws from her previous careers as an English teacher in Japan, custom boat builder salesperson and minor league baseball team representative, among others, to connect her lessons to real world applications. Ms. O'Brien credits her experiences as a military wife and teacher on a military installation for her flexibility, organizational skills, and high expectations of herself and her students.

Definition of Highly Effective Teaching

Ms. O'Brien defined highly effective teaching as "teaching to make kids think." She emphasized the importance of being able to think rather than simply memorize dates, facts, names, and places. She encourages her students to question what they read and to look at things "deeper and to put history in context." She further stated:

> They are bombarded with so much information today unlike when I was their age. Now, they have access to so much information; therefore I spend a lot of time talking about validity. It's important for them to know the facts first, and then they can form their opinion. Teaching kids to think for themselves is what highly effective teachers do no matter the subject.

Ms. O'Brien commented that highly effective teachers "have an ability to be empathetic to their students." She stated that it is wrong to eat or drink in front of students, "not because they're not allowed to eat in class but because we have kids here who may be hungry. How tortuous is it to sit and watch someone eat when you're hungry?" Ms. O'Brien also stressed the importance of caring. She said, "I'm old enough to be their grandparent but I try to somehow bond with them. They know I care about them. They know I'm on their side even if I'm angry with them." Ms. O'Brien recalled one of her previous students saying that she had "the nicest tone." She always wanted to be a teacher but said, "When I got out of college, I didn't teach for quite a while so what I learned there, I probably forgot." She further stated:

I think that I have a love of teaching and love of kids and in particular this age group. I have the skill to bond with these kids and yet I'm not a pushover. I have really good discipline but I think it's because they know that I want them to learn so badly. I think it's just a feeling of safety and being able to think and say what they think in my room.

Ms. O'Brien provided the following examples of highly effective teaching in her classroom: (a) higher order thinking skill questions, (b) organization, being prepared every day, (c) subject matter knowledge, (d) discipline and classroom management. She credited her success with classroom management on being prepared and organized. She pointed to the whiteboard and exclaimed:

Every day there's something up there to copy. They know where it is and what it is. Every day it explains what we're going to do and what they need so they're ready to go. When I say, "'this is for the turn in list," they know what I mean. When you come in here and you hear a lot of talking, it's productive talking and that's something that's taken me years to get used to...classrooms aren't quiet anymore. There is structure and the kids know that if they come in and I haven't put things on the board like occasionally happens, some know to go on and do exactly what they always do but some freeze for a second. But, there's also a trust there that they know that it's going to be ok. Structure is what's important at this age level.

Ms. O'Brien suggested that her students would describe a highly effective teacher as one who "makes stuff really interesting" and a classroom in which they are "never bored." "They always feel like they can contribute in here and that the class goes by so fast." She claimed that the best compliment she ever received and "took to heart the most" was when a student said, "I always feel so smart in here." She further stated, "One kid told me 'you're always happy to be here', so I think it goes back to those same things that I think are most important...caring and being empathetic."

Knowledge, Experiences, and Factors

When asked about factors that have contributed most to her development as a highly effective teacher, Ms. O'Brien credited getting certified and working in adult education and with the youth challenge program as a supervisor. Teaching at risk adults helped her as a point of reference now when she teaches at risk youth. She reflected, "I think that my formal education training was so long ago, I don't remember much from then. I think my life experiences have been most beneficial." She taught English to non-English learners in Japan during which she "learned a lot from that experience." Ms. O'Brien also credited her experience as a supervisor for a youth challenge program under the military department, where she worked her way up to the equivalent of a school's assistant principal, as invaluable. She claimed, "I had really good people I worked for who taught me a lot in that program." She continued discussing her life experiences by declaring, "My life experiences have made me a highly effective teacher, not formal education." She added, "I think that teachers are born, not made. I think there's a talent. You can learn the techniques, but if you don't love it and want to do it, all the techniques in the world aren't going to help you."

When asked about significant events that have contributed to her teaching success, Ms. O'Brien stated:

> My life has done that. I got married out of college to a guy who went to the Naval academy. We lived in Japan. I taught English there, we moved back and then I worked in retail. When we lived in Rhode Island, I worked for a sailboat company in which I was the liaison between custom boat makers and customers. I'd go to the engineer and explain what the customer wanted and determine the cost. I worked with the boat makers who were mostly Portuguese so again, communicating with non-English speaking people has helped me in communicating with middle school kids, trying to make things as clear as I can. Living overseas, I learned to be flexible. I've also worked for a minor league baseball team. My resume includes a lot of different experiences so when I talk to kids, I can refer to a lot of different things and I think that's what makes my class interesting.

Ms. O'Brien claimed that she has learned much from the many different supervisors, bosses and principals with whom she has worked. In addition to working with competent school administrators, she noted:

> I've had one or two really horrible principals and I've
> learned from them as well. I worked for a principal who, if
> it wasn't his idea, it wasn't good. We would intentionally
> drop a piece of paper in his office with an idea on it that we
> wanted in the school. The next week, it would be his idea
> and we'd get what we wanted. Teachers can be very
> creative when we need to be.

Practices and Methods

When asked about preparing high quality and rigorous lesson
plans in terms of setting instructional outcomes, Ms. O'Brien
replied while pointing to her lesson plan, "I'm an organized person
and I have everything that I do on here by topic and date."
However, in reference to lesson plans that are used for formal
observations, she exclaimed:

> I don't know how a teacher writes a lesson plan that tells
> somebody how a person's going to teach. They make us
> spend a lot of time on lesson plans. I'm not saying it's not
> important. I fortunately have a teaching partner who does a
> great job at writing lesson plans and she makes them look
> the way people want them to look nowadays. There's a
> higher order thinking question, there's what we do to
> modify for the sped [special education] kids, there's
> differentiation. But I'm really not a good lesson plan
> writer. I know what I want to accomplish and which
> topics, which points I want to cover. Those are in the

lesson plans. But, I could write my lesson plan on this day planner and I'd be the same teacher that I am with the lesson plan in that book that has to be out there every day. But, I understand why they require it so I do what I need to do. My lesson plans extend through the end of the month. They're printed out and for the most part, they're a guideline to make sure I stay on topic. I know what I want them to learn and that's what I do every day. I don't think I'm a good person to talk to about how to prepare a good lesson plan. It is what it is.

While Ms. O'Brien does not see herself as a "good lesson planner," she does believe that she has excellent classroom management skills. She emphasized, "Now *that* I have down." When discussing her classroom management philosophy, she explained:

One of the things I just had to learn was to breathe and go with the flow. They're not going to have everything you want them to have every day so the easiest thing is to just give it to them."

When I asked Ms. O'Brien to describe her daily classroom routine, she started by talking about a daily assignment in which important historical events of that date are reviewed:

I try to make it relevant to what we're studying that day but the calendar doesn't always cooperate. Some days, it's just a cultural thing I think they ought to know about. Some of these kids have never heard an Elvis or Sinatra song or have seen or know who Buddy Holly is. It's cultural stuff. But every day they come in and copy that and once a month we go through them and I give them a little quiz and it's just a matter of what happened on this day just to make sure they're doing it. That's their first job every day. They know where to pick stuff up and then we start the lesson. I always try to lead-in that way and then we go through the material. That's why procedure every day is important. I use a lot of music and video of the time when and where it's applicable. Finally, the powers that be last year gave us the freedom to use YouTube. A lot of times, that's how I end a lesson. I try to incorporate music. I find that's a really good way to get their attention and it helps them learn things. But every day starts with structure, with the same process every day."

Ms. O'Brien claimed that orchestrating high-level questioning and discussion is an area in which she still needs to improve. She explained that she only has her students for 47 minutes at a time and feels that while she may not have tried as much as she needs to, she has not had much success at grouping. She stated, "There are teachers here who are doing it and doing it well but their classes are blocked, English and math in particular with double class periods." She explained that instead of small groups, "we have conversations as a class." She described her questioning and discussion technique in the following manner:

In fact, I tell them not to raise their hand because I make it a point to call on the kid that might not know the answer and I love it when they say something that really adds to the conversation. One of the things that was hard for me to do that I've improved on recently is to give students an extended period of time to answer and make the class give them a chance to answer. You have high level students and low level students and I want that low level kid's voice to be heard as much as the high level kid and really they're kind of the same. They are both reluctant to raise their hands. The high level kids are afraid to show off and the low level kids are shy. By the end of the first grading period, I feel like all of my kids want to raise their hands. Maybe I'm not going about it right but I'm always willing to try. I tried grouping in fours with a smart and a middle smart and a middle low and a low [groups]. It just seems like my grandma used to say, "too much sugar for a dime." I don't want it to seem that I don't want to try new things because I do. I'm not that old person who won't change. My teaching methods have changed a lot over the years. I have questions I want them to think about and I'm going to ask them and then they can ask me questions and so when you say orchestrate, that word really throws me. How can you orchestrate what's going to come out of a middle-schooler's mouth? We go with where they take us. I have the beginning question and then we go where they take us. You have to allow time for that and develop trust for that. I am the conductor of the animal farm some days and my 8th hour class is the classic case. I have kids who are so smart and I have some that, bless their hearts...but even the *bless their hearts* ones will say something significant and when I give them assurance about what they said, they get more confident and excited.

Ms. O'Brien summarized her questioning philosophy by declaring, "You give them direction and you hope that's where they go but you're not orchestrating it, they orchestrate me, they tell me where to go, not the other way around."

When asked how she ensures that all students are engaged, Ms. Obrien pointed to a cup full of popsicle sticks and stated, "I start the year with those silly sticks that everyone laughs at but the first couple days they have fun, they make their own. So I start with that and they learn the process." She uses this process as a means of both randomly selecting students to provide input as well as keep them on their toes. She said, "I put their stick back in the cup after they answer a question so they see that they can't relax after they answer a question." When discussing how she keeps students engaged and paying attention, she explained, "During the first few weeks, some think I'm pretty mean because I'm pretty strict about how they do things and how they talk to each other." She told her students at the beginning of the school year in order to set the tone:

Once you come in my room, I only get you for 47 minutes and we don't have time to waste, so no, you can't go to the bathroom or get something you forgot, or a drink of water. Once you're in my room, you see what you need on the board and get busy because once that bell rings, we are going to start.

By the second nine weeks, most of her students tell her that hers is their favorite class. She added, "But, at the beginning they're scared of me." Ms. O'Brien believes in setting the ground rules early. She described how she does this:

I don't intentionally scare them, my tone doesn't change but I don't think they're used to having someone lay down the law and they don't realize that in those parameters there's a lot of leeway. I'm old school where I scare them the first month because it's easy after that. I'm not nearly like what I used to be but still I think there's some truth in that especially with students at this age level.

In a discussion regarding assessment and monitoring student learning, Ms. O'Brien stated, "I format all of my tests so that as much as possible, they're like the iLEAP or LEAP. The kids tell me my tests are really hard because I'm asking them to think. It's not a lot of parroting." She explained her reasoning for this approach, "When they get to the iLEAP, I want them to say that it was easy." In terms of informal assessing and monitoring student learning, she said, "It's just watching their growth. I assess them on a lot of things that are not based on their knowledge." Regarding how she assigns grades and monitors student learning, she offered:

We do some writing so there's some writing assessment in here. I also give them credit for when they organize their stuff, are prepared for class every day, and participate. When we're studying a unit, we have vocabulary words, graphs, maps, all of these things they need and then when the test comes they look for the study guide. I don't give them a study guide. They have the materials they need to study. I give them a list a turn in list of vocabulary words, maps, charts, writings, paintings, etc. I make them turn those artifacts in and they get a grade for turning it in. It's already worked, we've done it. It solves a couple of problems. It makes them realize that they're not just going to sit and memorize things in my class and what we do in class is important. I don't give much homework. I gave that up after two years here. You have one small group of kids who would really do it. Then you have kids whose parents do it, and a group of kids who won't do it.

Ms. O'Brien took pride in stating that no student has failed her class for the past two years. In fact, she said, "I tell them at the beginning of the year that it's as hard to fail my class as it is to make an A. I help them a lot, they can come in here during lunch and they can help each other."

Support Systems

When asked about how her administrator(s) prepared her for the Compass observations, Ms. O'Brien replied, "They stressed the higher order thinking questions a lot. They do not want to see teachers sitting behind their desk." With passionate conviction, she stated, "You can't sit behind your desk, you have to be engaged and the kids have to see the engagement." She explained the observation process:

> We had walk-throughs and I kind of enjoyed it. They noted if the objective was on the board. When they talked to a kid, they wanted to know if the student knew what the lesson was and why it was being done. That's the type of classroom they're looking for and want to see. They also told us that most of us are doing a good job and there was nothing to be nervous about, keep doing what you're doing and you'll be fine. There wasn't much of a stress level if you knew you were doing the best you could do and therefore you didn't have to worry about the observation. Again, they stressed engagement and higher order thinking questions.

When reflecting on the observation experience, Ms. O'Brien said, "That has changed a lot of the way that I teach to make sure that I do those things. It made me question, am I providing an opportunity for every kid to get it?" When asked about receiving feedback from pre- and post-observation conferences, Ms. O'Brien responded, "I think principals are under a lot of pressure. I don't think sometimes we get enough critical feedback." She believes administrators spend a lot of time with five to six teachers to "get them to an acceptable baseline." Therefore, she simply hears from her administrator, "You're doing great, keep doing what you're doing."

Ms. O'Brien claimed that of all of the professional development opportunities in which she has participated, Kagan strategies and Literacy Design Collaborative (LDC) have been the most beneficial in terms of preparing her for highly effective teaching. She acknowledged:

> The Kagan strategies, as much as I don't like grouping, you don't have to put them in groups to do some of those things. We have workshops and lots of training in Kagan and I think it has helped with higher order questioning techniques. I have also learned a lot by being a part of LDC, even though I don't feel like I can do it to the extent that they would like me to. I think I underestimate my kids sometimes when it comes to primary source materials and I think LDC has helped me utilize more of that. Students won't use the dictionary book so I got to thinking about it...I don't use the phone book anymore, I use my iPhone. So, when we received some technology money, I bought 15 hand held electronic dictionaries and they'll use those. I just have to be careful to chunk it and where it's helped the most is using the electronic dictionaries. Words are so important and their vocabulary is sometimes very limited. I'm doing a better job of letting them look at primary sources and saying 'you read this and tell me what it says' and it's amazing at what they can do when using those electronic dictionaries. Kagan, LDC, primary sources,

higher order thinking skills trainings have been most beneficial.

Upon reflecting on what she needed from local and state levels of education in order to maintain highly effectiveness, Ms. O'Brien declared, "Money"! She reasoned:

> During the summer, students have too much idle time to get into trouble and learn unproductive habits. We should have school year-round to keep them active and involved in learning. When I was younger, my mother was a stay at home mom and she made sure that we continued to read and learn during the summer months, but the world has changed. Many kids are at home by themselves during the summer. So much of the way we do things in society has changed but the school year hasn't. In that respect, I hate when the summer months get here because they're just going to go sit in front of the TV all summer if they're lucky. They can't work, they're too young, their parents don't have resources to send them to summer camp, some will fend for themselves. So, when I say money, I'm not talking just about increasing teacher salaries, I'm talking about adequate supplies and increasing the time kids spend in school.

She concluded by offering, "Of course, a better salary would also keep highly effective teachers from either moving into administration for more money or out of education altogether."

6. MS. MILLER

Ms. Miller has been a classroom teacher for 12 years. She currently teaches three sections of 5th grade science and one section of 5th grade social studies. She formerly taught 5th and 6th grade math, science and social studies for two years at her current school. In a previous school, she taught all subjects in 1st and 2nd grades for five years. She also has experience with teaching kindergarteners for half of a year. She obtained her bachelor's and master's degrees from a regional university in north Louisiana. She is certified to teach first through eighth grades and also holds a provisional principal certification. The school at which she taught during the 2013-2014 school year is located in a rural area where 50% of the student population qualified for free or reduced lunch. Ms. Miller's personality exudes energy and enthusiasm. She cited her experiences as a young teacher at a Montessori school as being one of the main factors of her current classification as a highly effective teacher.

Definition of Highly Effective Teaching

Ms. Miller defined highly effective teacher as one who

"knows the students, has knowledge of the concepts, and a deep understanding of the standards." She expanded on her definition by including:

> Teaching your heart out. Always being here, always being prepared, being on time, being organized. Knowing what is expected of me and what I need to teach and how my students learn by using different data to come up with their weaknesses and strengths. Knowing from past experiences as a teacher, my strength and weaknesses and getting into best practices and finding out what is going to reach my students in order to get them the skills they need.

Ms. Miller believes that a highly effective teacher has a sincere passion for teaching and is not simply in it for the summer break. She knew from when she was a kindergartner that she wanted to be a teacher. She further declared:

> Teaching is my passion, my calling. I'm enthusiastic, energetic and willing to find out what I'm doing wrong, willing to do the research, long hours, whatever I need to do to reach my students. I put a lot of time and effort into it. You have to be organized, present, and on time on a daily basis. I strive to do those things. I try hard to be here on time, stay late, make sure I'm always at school because a substitute, while they're great, they can't teach like I can. You have to be fair and consistent with discipline. If the kids know that you love them and are there for them and you're going to be consistent and fair, they'll do what

they're supposed to do because you set the bar and they'll meet it.

Ms. Miller commented that her students would describe her as "fun." She commented, "A lot of them would say they love me or I know that she cares about me or I'm consistent and fair." She explained that her students would probably mention that in being consistent, every student would receive the same consequences regardless of who they are. She also said that her students would describe her as "energetic, enthusiastic, happy, and organized."

Knowledge, Experiences, and Factors

When Ms. Miller first entered the education profession, her first teaching job was in a Montessori school in central Louisiana. Going into that position, she recalled, "I didn't know anything about Montessori. I was a novice teacher making a lot of mistakes." When asked to further explain her experiences during her years at the Montessori school, she offered:

> I went through the training to be Montessori certified and began to learn about what a hands on, child centered classroom looks like and how to differentiate your lessons for high [level] and low [level] students. I really think those years that I spent at that school helped me to become the teacher that I am now because it forced me to differentiate. I had 1st and 2nd grade with low and high achieving students. There were no desks, a new curriculum, no textbooks, no teacher manuals. I really had to dive into those GLEs [Grade Level Expectations]

because I had no book that told me what to teach and how to teach it. I went through the GLEs [Grade Level Expectations] with my Montessori curriculum. I learned what to teach, when to teach and how to teach. That experience helped me become what I am today because I had to get my classroom management and lesson planning under control.

When asked about individuals who have contributed to her becoming a highly effective teacher, Ms. Miller recalled a former colleague from the Montessori school. She explained that at that particular school, there were no doors or permanent walls. She elaborated:

The lady that taught next to me had much more experience and was a master teacher. She took me under her wing and we opened up that curtain. I was able to see how she modeled lessons with her students, how she used those Montessori materials as well as how she planned lessons. We planned everything together. Being able to have someone like her helped because she modeled classroom management, how to use the materials, how to plan lessons, how to run a classroom where everyone is doing something different and it's not just teacher centered. She was the greatest influence.

Ms. Miller summarized her time spent at her former school as an experience that was "invaluable." She pointed out that had she not moved because of her husband's job, she would still be teaching there now. However, she went on to say, "I love it here too though. It's been good for me to take what I learned at the Montessori school and apply it here." She stated that even though she no longer has access to the Montessori manipulatives and resources, she's been able to "adjust and make it work." Ms. Miller also credits her husband and mother for helping at home so that she has time to grade papers and stay late at school when necessary. She concluded our conversation regarding positive influences by saying:

> I firmly think that God called me to be a teacher. He gave me the passion. I pray over my students. I don't pray with them, but over them so I feel like God is in my classroom helping me do what I need to do.

Practices and Methods

When asked about preparing high quality and rigorous lesson plans in terms of setting instructional outcomes, Ms. Miller replied:

> First, I go through what it is that I want to teach. I go through the GLEs [Grade Level Expectations] and decide what I need to teach for the year. Then, I go through whatever resources I have in hand. I go through the textbook, pull resources from the internet and other books I have in the classroom. Then, I start looking at the observation rubric. I know what I need to do. I must have an objective on the wall and state it so the kids understand it. I look at that rubric as I'm planning out the lesson to be

sure that I hit all of the things that I need to have in there. I make sure to include higher order thinking questions and technology when lesson planning. So, I start with the GLEs [Grade Level Expectations] and then I find resources and then as I begin to build the lesson plan, I focus on the rubric and think of the best teaching practices to use.

She explained that she tries to make use of every available minute at school planning because she has young children at home. She claimed that she spends "little time in the teacher's lounge or in the hall visiting." She further stated, "My goal here is to do what I need to do for my job. We have 30 minutes to an hour depending on what day it is for break time during the school day." She reported that it takes her an entire week to write lesson plans for the following week. However, one day per week, she is unable to plan for her science class, "because we're team meeting and I'm planning social studies so I'm actually using four days to plan for science." Regarding how she manages her time at school and in the classroom, she elaborated:

Sometimes, I have to do some planning and grading before school. I stay late one day a week for about 45 minutes to catch up. Grading papers is done at home at night after my kids go to bed and on the weekends. I try to do most of my lesson planning at school. I don't grade papers during class time.

When asked about her classroom routines and procedures, Ms. Miller said that every student has a job and they know what is expected. She takes pride in saying that her classroom runs with very little guidance. She explained:

> I try to run my classroom so that it runs without me being there. I believe that classroom management is not just making them behave. It's about a set of procedures that you have in your classroom. Students like consistency and routine. At the beginning of the school year, we go through the whole PBIS set of rules at school and talk about what they look like. We write our own rules and discuss the expectations. I set up a lot of routines such as how to sharpen their pencil, go to the restroom, get tissue. Then we talk about how to handle materials in the science lab and the jobs that each student has.
>
> Being respectful and all of those things line up for the rest of the year and I have to be consistent for it to run smoothly. They know there are consequences for negative behavior. I have very little disrespect because they know I respect them. I don't yell and scream because I don't think that's needed. They know when I'm upset without having to raise my voice. We set up transitions like how to line up in the hallway, get books out, get ready for the next activity. We're constantly moving, discussing, taking notes, conducting a hands-on activity or watching a video clip. I know that if I don't' keep them engaged, that's when we have behavior problems. They're focused on science and aren't thinking about how they can misbehave.

She advised, "When they're not engaged and when you're not organized and don't' have management techniques in place, that's when you'll have problems."

Orchestrating high-level questioning and discussion is an area in which she must plan ahead, but Ms. Miller admitted she struggles at times getting her young students to participate in a meaningful discussion. She said, "I have to write the questions down because if I don't write the HOT [higher order thinking] questions down, I'll forget to ask them." When asked to elaborate on her questioning methods, she offered:

> I write two or three questions while I'm lesson planning. Sometimes during the course of the class, I'll think of something else that may be a good question based on something a student says or asks. We have a question and discussion time during class in which they try to build their skills of meaningful discussion. It is a hard skill to learn in 5th grade because they don't want to discuss with me much less than with each other. They're scared of saying something wrong. They don't want to say, "Well, I think something different." Nobody wants to be wrong so we're having to work through those skills of how to have a meaningful discussion.
>
> I try to gear my hands on activities to have a HOT part to them where they're having to create something or evaluate or analyze something or compare and contrast. With the new observation rubric, you have to do a lot of

discussion. A lot of that tends to be teacher guided because kids aren't ready yet to discuss. In middle school and high school, they have their own thoughts and know how to communicate them but at the elementary level, they're not ready for that. They look to you to see if it's the right answer. They won't say anything else until you validate their answer. I have to use techniques to turn it so that it becomes more child-centered.

When asked how she ensures that all students are engaged, Ms. Miller emphasized the key is in keeping students' attention by incorporating a variety of interesting and fun activities in her lessons with seamless transitions. She elaborated:

I try to spend a minimal amount of time on each thing so that they're always moving to different activities because when you're lecturing for 30 minutes they start dozing off. You do need a little bit of whole class instruction because they need to know what they're going to do in the centers. I have to constantly change activities so we're never in the same activity for a long time. I use activities in which they move, not just their hands, but their body as well. Getting up and moving to the next desk or doing a jumping jack or something that has them moving has an effect on keeping them engaged.

I like making the activities fun. They like to laugh and I like to laugh too so we tell some science jokes. I tell them stories about my kids, we laugh and joke and that keeps them engaged. I try really hard to integrate all of the subjects (art, drawing, writing, singing, athletics, games, reading comprehension) into the activities. Even though I'm not the English teacher, I'm still teaching those skills to them. I have nonfiction texts that fall in line with common core standards so I'm pulling in all those skills they need in their reading class.

Ms. Miller summarized her method of student engagement by emphasizing that she is a "hands-on teacher." She described her classroom as one that is "a child centered environment in which students make choices of what they need to do and how they learn." She continued, "We have stations that are hands on and they have choices in terms of order and how they set up their experiment to reach their scientific goals. Some set them up differently."

In a discussion regarding assessment and monitoring of student learning, Ms. Miller noted that she begins each school year with a science inventory questionnaire of her students during which they "talk about their interests in science." In terms of monitoring student learning, she commented, "I look at their previous year's LEAP scores. I look at their weaknesses and make note of those when we get to that content area." When the topic shifted to assessments, she elaborated:

We take chapter tests based on the textbook which is based on common core. It covers all the GLEs [Grade Level Expectations], it's awesome. I've never had a book as great as it is...there are discussion questions, good experiments, it's a great resource! I base my summative assessments on those chapters. If one or more students totally miss a concept, then I need to go back and either pull that one child or teach the whole class for whatever reason and re-teach that concept. In between, during every lesson, I use formative assessments such as thumbs up/down. We write answers on student white boards. I formatively assess their discussion questions, participation, and stations. They have to record everything they do whether it's reading comprehension or they're actually designing an experiment.

A lot of times they don't recognize words seen on state testing, therefore we have to work on vocabulary. We use exit cards at the end of the day to tell me what they learned, didn't learn, they rate themselves. Those things really help me during the course of the lesson because sometimes you have to change your lesson for the next day. If they didn't get it, there's no sense in continuing. With science, as far as standardized test prep, there's very little out there. We spend our time instead focusing on mastering skills. We talk about how to look at a question and process that information, how to cross out, how to draw pictures, how to reason if you don't exactly know the answer. I look at how they scored on the iLEAP to plan for how I'll improve the following year by noting the concepts in which they were weak. From that data, I focus on what I can do better. I chart it each year, making note of the areas in which I need to improve.

Support Systems

When asked how her administrator(s) prepared her for the Compass observations, Ms. Miller indicated that she had a significant amount of meaningful training, support, and preparation. She explained:

> We had several faculty meeting sessions in which they went through the rubric at the beginning of the year so we had time to study it and start planning lessons. They showed us videos of highly effective and ineffective teaching so that we could see what it looks like and what it doesn't look like. They emphasized student choice in the rubric. They made it clear about what they were going to look for and gave us some ideas to use. They gave us opportunities to practice with them about what they were looking for before the actual observations.

Reflecting on the observation experience, Ms. Miller recalled that last year she met with both the principal and assistant principal and they both conducted the formal observation. She stressed how important it was to meet with them before the observation to discuss or describe unique situations in terms of student needs and behaviors. Ms. Miller sincerely valued the post-observation feedback she received. She explained:

> I was able to tell them about how the kids had jobs and they already know what to do. I was able to tell them about

what they're going to see so that during the stations, if they don't make it around to each station, they know what's going on in all the stations. After the observation, they gave some ideas on how to improve or do things differently and I like that because no one is perfect. There's always room to improve. I'm not perfect but I want to be! It's great for someone else to give you feedback because no one can think of everything. It's good to have a set of fresh eyes giving you ideas on how to improve.

Ms. Miller claimed that of all the professional development opportunities in which she has participated, Montessori trainings were "without a doubt, the best." She also went through the Louisiana Teacher Assistance and Assessment Program (LATAAP) mentor training. She described her LATAAP training as one that "made it clear about what the state department identified as effective teaching." She has also attended various sessions on whole brain instructional theory and a leadership academy. She gleaned from the leadership academy the importance of credibility and respect. She acknowledged that a good principal has to be able to offer credible ideas to teachers on how to improve their practices or methods. Additionally, she noted that "people want to do well for people they look up to, respect, and are there to help them."

Upon reflecting on what she needed from local and state levels of education in order to maintain highly effectiveness, Ms. Miller declared, "More training in best practices." She recalled a situation in which she wanted to attend a state science conference but, "there were no funds to send me and I couldn't afford to pay my own way." She added:

> Unfortunately, there's a lack of funds for training opportunities and it would be nice if there were more funds for that. We need to be learning all the time. We constantly need to be exposed to new practices and ideas.

Ms. Miller also expressed a desire for "training in the areas that need improvement on the observation rubric. It would be nice for them to give us ideas, strategies, techniques, samples of lesson plans, etc. that would help in the areas of the rubric." She spends a lot of time on the internet, Pinterest, and instructional blogs looking for ways to improve questioning and discussion which she noted, "is my weakest area." She recommended, "Maybe have opportunities to be paired with a teacher who does something well that you have a weakness in." She is hopeful that the state department, "will look at the Compass data to see where strengths and weaknesses across the state are and set up professional development opportunities to help in the weaker areas."

7. MS. LANE

Ms. Lane has been in education for 20 years. She currently teaches 5th grade math, science, and social studies. She obtained her bachelor's and master's degree from a regional university in southeast Louisiana. She is certified to teach first through eighth grades regular education and K-12 special education. The school at which she taught during the 2013-2014 school year is located in a suburban area where 68% of the student population qualified for free or reduced lunch. Ms. Lane credits her personal experiences as a mother of a child with a severe learning disability for the patience, compassion, and desire needed to help all children reach their academic potential.

Definition of Highly Effective Teaching

Ms. Lane defined highly effective teaching as a condition in which "all of the students reach their potential and walk out of the classroom an independent learner." She further described a highly effective teacher as one who possesses humility and intuition. She elaborated:

> You have to be humble and someone who loves kids and everything that comes with it. You need to be aware of the

student's needs. They're all different with different needs. You must have a willingness to go above and beyond, great management skills, and knowledge of the subject content. It's also important to have the ability to plan, deliver that plan effectively, have structure but with a sense of humor.

When describing her style of teaching, Ms. Lane claimed "the students are 100% engaged. I teach in a scaffolding approach. There's a lot of higher order thinking in my classroom. It's important for them to understand the content rather than memorize it." Ms. Lane further described herself as "very spontaneous," and added, "They'll run with an idea and I'll go with them as long as they're learning." She has "high expectations for my students and myself." Her students "self-monitor their progress and effort levels." In fact, one of the most satisfying aspects of teaching is "to see intrinsic motivation in my students," she noted. "I see a big shift towards higher order thinking, more effort, more diligence." Ms. Lane said, "and a deeper knowledge of the curriculum more so than ever."

Ms. Lane commented that her students would describe her as "someone who is funny but strict." Additionally, she claimed her students would say that she is "fair." She expounded:

> They want someone who makes learning fun, interesting, and applies lesson content to their lives. I think they like me. A lot of them appreciate me because I do push them to a higher level. They appreciate the fact that I teach for understanding rather than just rote memorization.

Knowledge, Experiences, and Factors

When asked about factors that have contributed most to her development as a highly effective teacher, Ms. Lane exclaimed, "I've always had a sense or knowledge of the curriculum. I've always taught for understanding, not simply just getting through the lesson." Her background in special education is "a major factor because the techniques used in special education apply to all students." She additionally cited her experience of earning a national board certification. She recalled:

> When I went through the [teacher national board] certification process, it makes you look at yourself from every angle. It was a tough experience but it forces you to analyze yourself as a teacher and makes you aware of every aspect of teaching because of the way it's designed.

When asked about significant events that have contributed to her teaching success, Ms. Lane referred to workshops in which the common core standards were "unpacked" as well as "lots of workshops on higher order thinking with Bloom's Taxonomy." She noted that workshops on differentiated instruction "have been very beneficial." "However," Ms. Lane stated, "The one that stands out the most is an in-service in which we learned how to write in different subject areas using academic vocabulary."

When asked about individuals who have contributed to her becoming a highly effective teacher, Ms. Lane proudly and without hesitation stated, "My students, their parents and my peers, but most importantly, my students. I learn so much from them." She reflected on a pivotal time in her life before she became a teacher:

> My son has a severe learning disability. When I was trying to teach him to read, other parents asked me to help their kids to read also. I went to a workshop at which I was highly intimidated, but there was a wonderful principal from Lafourche parish who was my partner who told me, "Honey, you're wonderful, you need to go into teaching. I did and I swore that none of my students would go through what my son went through."

Practices and Methods

When asked about preparing high quality and rigorous lesson plans in terms of setting instructional outcomes, Ms. Lane emphasized the importance of being very familiar with the subject standards and explained:

> The first thing I do is unpack the standards. You have to be very familiar with the standards. Then, I determine how I'm going to approach it, and put it in sequential order. Then, I prepare my lessons. We don't have a lot of resources. I make my own plans. There are a few things I can find but I'm not by the book at all. They're more in my head than anything. I'm not real formal with lesson plans. It's usually in a notebook or on a piece of paper. I could write one that is formal but I wouldn't even look at it. I know what I need to do. I know what I have to teach. I just kind of go with it. Whatever the concept is, I want them to fully understand it. For observations, I write a

picture perfect one. I can make it look nice and neat.

When we discussed her classroom management philosophy, Ms. Lane noted that she invests time at the beginning of the school year talking with her students about the importance of gaining a quality education. She commented:

They learn at the beginning of the school year. We sit down and talk about why we're here. They get a behavior chart that eventually fades out because it's not needed after a few weeks because they get used to the routine. I don't have a lot of discipline problems. I tell them what I expect. If they don't do what they're supposed to do, there are consequences, if they do what they're supposed to do, they get privileges.

Ms. Lane claimed that orchestrating high-level questioning and discussion is an important aspect of guiding her students to being critical thinkers and not just memorizers. She described:

At the beginning of the year, I actually show them Bloom's Taxonomy at a kid level. They see the difference between LOT [lower order thinking] and HOT [higher order thinking]. So, they understand that in a discussion, we don't just call out things; we want to have a meaningful discussion. We do an activity called stop/swap, turn/talk. We do it at the beginning and they actually have to write about what we discussed in their journal. After they finish writing, they swap. They can't be critical, they can criticize, but not in a mean way. They just have to point out what was good or what was misunderstood and then they turn and talk about it. From there, whatever lends itself to a discussion, we go with. Sometimes I have to intervene because they'll want to talk for the whole class period. Sometimes it's like pulling teeth, other times it's easy. But it's spontaneous more than anything.

Ms. Lane said that she has tried a Socratic seminar, "but it took up too much instructional time. I'd rather have two to three shorter discussions that are productive than one big one that eats up too much time."

When asked how she ensures that all students are engaged, Ms. Lane emphatically stated, "I'm a stickler for that." She pointed out how important it is to acquire and maintain student attention and focus throughout a class period. She elaborated:

> They know that if they're not paying attention, they better at least look like they're paying attention. I use a lot of eye contact. If I lose their eye contact, I just stop. Once they don't hear me talking, they'll refocus and look at me. When they're working on an activity or a turn and talk, I'm always walking around to monitor. I ask a lot of questions. I'll ask them to repeat what other students say and that keeps them on their toes. My goal is to get them to work independently. I work at it real hard at the beginning and then once it kicks in, my job is easy.

In a discussion regarding assessment and monitoring student learning, Ms. Lane expressed concern with district-wide, mandated assessments by saying, "Benchmark math tests are dictated by the district. The tests are generated by a computer program but they don't always go along with the content." In terms of how students are otherwise assessed formally in her classes, she explained:

> Tests are broken down into units. I also use self-made assessments. I do allow students to retake tests sometimes where I'll take an average of the two. Or, sometimes I allow an alternative assessment such as an essay.

Regarding formative assessment, she stated, "I ask a lot of informal questions to see if they're paying attention."

Support Systems

When asked about how her administrator(s) prepared her for the Compass observations, Ms. Lane replied, "She called us all in and told us what they would be looking for and gave us the rubric. We talked about the components and what they meant along with examples of what they should look like." When reflecting on the observation experience, Ms. Lane said:

> She had nothing but good things to say. In all reality, did I deserve the four? I don't know, maybe I did, maybe I didn't. She was very enthused because the kids were engaged and learning and I was doing all the right things."

When asked what she needed from local and state levels of education in order to maintain highly effective rating, Ms. Lane was less than optimistic that she would maintain her highly effective status. She reasoned:

> I don't feel that it's going to happen this year because first

of all, the state department told us we're not getting VAM [value-added model]scores, we'll get SLT [student learning target] scores. We were told by the parish we had to put 85% of our students will score basic or above. I said no, I'm not doing that. They said you have to. I have kids who have never scored basic before. It's going to be almost impossible for those kids to score basic. I have a lot of kids who are SPED [special education] and they'll grow, but not that much.

The SLTs [student learning targets] are based on the iLEAP [integrated Louisiana educational assessment program]. VAM [value-added model] scores measure progress or growth which is actually a more accurate indicator of teacher effectiveness. The district told us exactly what to put on it and that's not the way SLTs [student learning targets] are supposed to be designed. You're supposed to analyze your data and based on that, you're supposed to set your goals. The second reason is that this year, I have a different observer, and she told us all that no one would be rated highly effective. She gave me a 3.4 but that's not important to me. I'm just interested in my students' learning.

Ms. Lane expressed concern with the amount of time students are pulled from her classes for a variety of non-instructional purposes. She would like for the value-added model to take into account the number of instructional minutes missed by students.

She pointed out that in some cases, "students are not marked absent because they're actually at school, but may have been pulled from her class for a variety of reasons." Additionally, in reference to instructional time, Ms. Lane stated that, "The [state standardized] test needs to be pushed back to May so we're not so much in a hurry and are able to teach at a deeper level." She concluded by offering, "I consider myself a highly effective teacher...not because of those VAM scores or the observations, but because I do my job every day. My kids are learning."

8. MS. FRANKLIN

Ms. Franklin has been in education for five years. For the past four years, she has taught and is currently teaching, math, science and social studies to fourth graders. During her first year in education, she taught third grade math, social living and spelling. She earned her bachelor's and master's degree from a regional university in southwest Louisiana. She is certified to teach first through fifth grades and also possesses a certification in school administration. The school at which she taught during the 2013-2014 school year is located in a rural setting where 45% of the student population qualified for free or reduced lunch. She exhibits a strong work ethic as well as an unsurpassed level of dedication to her students.

Definition of Highly Effective Teaching

Ms. Franklin defined highly effective teaching as being "student-centered, well-rounded, and knowledgeable of subject content." She emphasized the importance of planning for, and facilitating student-led activities in which the students have responsibilities. She claimed highly effective teachers learn from their peers. Ms. Franklin commented, "They need to have a good grasp of how their students learn. They motivate their students and promote a safe environment in which they feel comfortable discussing." She added that having effective classroom management is vital. When discussing examples of highly effective teaching in her classroom, she responded:

> Everything is student led. It takes us a little bit to get going but eventually, the students learn to pick their own groups, they pick the people with whom they'll have the best discussions. In our math centers, there's always a leader, there's always someone critiquing others. When they both get stuck, that's when I come in. I'm really just a facilitator.

Because of her role as a teacher leader, Ms. Franklin is able to frequently observe other highly effective teachers. She noted, "We're doing a lot of Kagan here which is really getting them into cooperative learning and more discussion." Her coworkers "utilize songs before they start poetry to get them engaged and excited about it rather than simply saying, 'this is a poem where things rhyme'." Ms. Franklin said that her students would describe her as "a teacher who cares for them and their learning, who takes the time to plan activities that they're interested in." She added, "one who allows them to take responsibility for their own learning."

Knowledge, Experiences, and Factors

When asked about factors that have contributed most to her development as a highly effective teacher, without hesitation Ms. Franklin responded, "I think I have a strong work ethic. I am very work minded all of the time." She indicated that she had been well prepared for the new Compass evaluation measurements and had in fact, already begun implementing most of the observation rubric requirements for highly effective teaching. She explained:

> Whenever the new compass observation rubric and common core standards came out, I looked at the rubric and analyzed what it was expecting of us. I noticed I was already doing a lot of that anyway because I don't like to sit and listen to someone talk for two hours so my nine and ten year olds surely don't want to sit and listen to me talk for two hours. When the rubric came out, I reflected on what I was already doing versus what I needed to do and thought about what I needed to do to get there. It wasn't so overwhelming. We were already doing it; we just needed to take it a step further.

> Last year, I really shifted more of the learning responsibilities on the students. In math, there has to be whole group instruction from the teacher, there's no getting around that. In the introduction of a new skill, it was me. Then it was them; and they're coming up with better ideas on how to explain it to each other.

When asked about significant events that have contributed to her teaching success, Ms. Franklin cited teacher leader conferences where "we could talk with other people from across the state" to discuss instructional strategies. She elaborated:

> It was eye opening because we shared successes and

struggles and we were able to take that back with us. When we took the reading and language standards and unpacked them, it helped to implement reading in science and social studies. It helped me to understand the standards better. That was very beneficial.

Ms. Franklin also recognized her coworkers for contributing to her teaching success and said, "We bounce ideas off each other. Whatever she's doing in reading, I try to pull it into science and social studies and she'll pull my science and social studies into her lessons."

Practices and Methods

When asked about preparing high quality and rigorous lesson plans in terms of setting instructional outcomes, Ms. Franklin replied, "I work backwards. I look at my assessments, and especially test items that are released by the state." She described her planning process:

> Being a teacher in the LEAP [Louisiana Educational Assessment Program] year, I think about which skills have not been taught yet to get us where we need to be. The lesson activities are designed with students being able to think for themselves. Then, I'll look back at the standard to make sure everything is aligned. I can't plan too far in advance. Lesson plans are due on Monday so I put them together on Thursday and Friday although I come up on Sundays a lot to finalize them. It probably takes me about an hour to an hour and a half to plan for the week.

When discussing her classroom management procedures, Ms. Franklin stated, "From the very beginning, the first day, our routines go into effect." She emphasized the importance of a structured, yet student-led environment in which students take responsibility for key classroom procedures. She explained:

> From the first day, we established how we would talk and interact with each other. It's all student led. They come in, set the timer, they get their stuff, they take turns putting things up. They like structure. They know every day that I'm going to teach from five to ten minutes or so and then it's on to an activity of some sort where they're required to give feedback to each other or interact with each other.
>
> Looking at the Danielson rubric, when we analyzed it before the school year started, everything was focused on a student led classroom. I thought hard about how to get fourth graders to do all of these things. I was really nervous at first but once they get in a routine, they like their responsibility. It gives them a purpose and lets them know that everyone is relevant.

Ms. Franklin pointed out, "Even before the Danielson rubric observations, what I did in my observations is what I do on a normal day." She commented, "They're not going to just perform how you want them to during an observation if it's not routine." When asked about how she approaches students who occasionally get off task, she replied:

> Distractions happen. At first I'll get down on their level

and talk with them about making better choices. Then I have a clipboard on which I mark and they don't want that to happen because it'll affect their PBIS reward. It goes back to the beginning of school when the expectations are cleared and they understand that if those expectations aren't followed, then there's consequences. The beginning is where the groundwork is laid.

Ms. Franklin claimed that high-level questioning and discussion are a common occurrence in her classroom. However, she stressed that it requires time, practice and patience to orchestrate. She explained:

It's a lot of modeling at first. If a student notices that his or her partner is struggling, we don't want to see them struggle so they start asking questions such as, "What do you think about doing it a different way, can we think of it differently?" It's teaching them to think differently. In fourth grade, I would say by late November, they're able to ask those questions and start thinking on that higher level. They practice and get better throughout the year. When I can actually cut back on the modeling and say, "What do I expect to hear?" They'll say, "Good questions. Good discussions."

When asked how she ensures that all students are engaged, Ms. Franklin commented, "They all have a job so I guess that's where cooperative learning comes in." She described dividing students into groups of four or five in which every student has a job and further explained:

> We have a coordinator who monitors the time. We do a lot
> of activities with marker boards, so they'll say, "Let's
> switch marker boards. Let's talk. Let's look at someone
> else's marker boards." Someone is in charge of getting
> materials and putting them up. Some are in charge of part
> of the activity.

When asked to elaborate on the activities, Ms. Franklin offered,
"The activities are relevant to them. For example, I incorporate
video games they're interested in. They actually designed one of
the centers during an activity on area and perimeter." She
emphasized that students "create their own questions." With a
sense of pride and accomplishment, she added, "As each team
rotates to each center, they're answering the questions generated by
their classmates."

When asked to discuss how she monitors student learning, Ms.
Franklin said that she particularly likes using Accelerated Math
[math software program], "because it addresses all the necessary
skills at this grade level." Regarding summative assessments in
her classroom, she stated:

> Informally, they assess themselves. I have a parking lot
> which is a place on the board where they can continuously
> give me feedback. They tell me good and bad things on
> there. I don't look at it until after class so during the
> Accelerated math time the next day, gives me about fifteen
> minutes to work one-on-one with them to address all those

issues. They'll even say, "Can I help someone? I really understand." We do "I can" statements on the board so whenever they can do it, they initial their name which is a way to show others in the class that if they need help, they can help.

Ms. Franklin explained that her formal assessments are carefully designed and timed. She stressed the importance of assessing her students only after she feels they're ready. She reasoned:

> They're tested so much. I wait until they're ready. I give formal assessments at the end of each standard that I teach. It's not really set. It's when I feel like they're ready. I don't rush a test just because I have to get a grade in. We test when I feel they're ready. My tests include multiple choice, explaining, and written expression. Sometimes I allow them to retake tests based on when the majority of the class struggles, which means they weren't ready. I then reflect on what I did or didn't do and then we come back and do it a different way and hopefully the second way is more effective. However, the need for retesting doesn't happen often.

Support Systems

When asked about how her administrator(s) prepared her for the Compass observations, Ms. Franklin explained:

> We were given the rubric before the school year started. We went over the rubric, each part extensively. We were

given time to talk with our coworkers within our grade

levels and other grade levels about how we would do this.

When asked about the observation process, she remarked, "I really

like the pre-observation conference because it makes you think

about your lesson before it happens."   Regarding post

observation conferences, she stated, "I really like the feedback

because if I'm not doing what I need to be doing to hit all those

points, then I need to adjust something." She recalled:

> In my first observation, I had one student who was not
>
> actively engaged the whole time. Afterwards I took the
>
> advice and thought, "How can I get him more involved and
>
> give him more responsibility? That's really what he
>
> wanted. He wanted that coordinator role. It really makes
>
> you reflect on how to improve what you're doing to get
>
> better.

Ms. Franklin claimed that of all of the professional

development opportunities in which she has participated, "The

most beneficial is just collaboration between all of us teachers."

She declared:

> Everyone has really good ideas. It's just making the time,
>
> which is hard during the day. Taking the time to talk and
>
> share is important. I talk with teachers across the hall to
>
> see how they're teaching different lessons. We have a
>
> strong support system in place with our administration who
>
> always has an open door for anytime we have questions or
>
> concerns. They're more than willing to help.

Upon reflecting on what she needed from local and state levels of education in order to maintain highly effectiveness, Ms. Franklin responded, "I think there needs to be a system of accountability." However, she stated, "It's going to be tough to maintain." She reasoned:

> We're not getting VAM scores for the next couple of years but there's so many factors to getting that level. The state's going to have to give us more information; more direction as far as what the problems on the test will look like. More sample test items need to be released. There's too much unknown regarding the PARCC. It's new and I guess it's unknown to them too. The students play a big part in a teacher being highly effective. The kids I have this year are different from the kids I had last year. They have to want to extend further than what we're doing. I can do everything I did last year; they can give the same exact test; and my kids this year might not perform as well. You don't know because they're different kids.

Ms. Franklin concluded by offering, "Our district is doing a lot to help. They're pulling in people from outside our parish to come in and talk with us to show us what different strategies look like. Professional development is always needed, it never stops."

9. MS. LOGAN

Ms. Logan has been in education for 16 years. She has experience in teaching at the kindergarten, first, second, third, and fourth grade levels. She is currently on sabbatical while working on her master's degree from a regional university in northwest Louisiana. She plans to return to the classroom as a fourth grade English teacher. Ms. Logan obtained her bachelor's degree from a regional university in southwest Louisiana. She is certified to teach pre-Kindergarten through eighth grade. The school at which she taught during the 2013-2014 school year is located in an urban area where 49% of the student population qualified for free or reduced lunch.

Ms. Logan admitted that the start of her teaching career was a stressful one in which she doubted her ability to teach. In fact, after her first year of teaching, she resigned, and worked briefly in a non-educational profession until she was called by a principal to come back and give it one more chance. As a teacher who earned a highly effective rating and perfect Compass evaluation score, her decision to re-enter the teaching profession has resulted in a quality education for her students.

Definition of Highly Effective Teaching

Ms. Logan defined highly effective teaching as, "a vocation, a calling." She said with passion and conviction, "It starts with the self. Your personal being. I see teaching as a call of duty, not as a job." She described effective teachers as those who "constantly reflect on practices in the classroom and try to identify weaknesses and strengths and figure out what to do to get better." She continued:

> You have to have the right attitude. A lot of teachers have a negative attitude and think that they can't, but I think any teacher can be highly effective because there are certain patterns that highly effective teachers practice and if you shift your beliefs towards those, then anybody can do it. You have to be a proactive learner. You can't just sit back and wait for the district to train you. Before Compass and Common Core, I started looking for better instructional strategies, because I knew I needed to constantly improve. I have been teaching sixteen years so my original practices were old school. I've always been a reflective person, thinking there's got to be a better way.

Ms. Logan advised, "You have to identify problems and seek solutions. Teach the students, not programs." She claimed to be "self-disciplined" and acknowledged that she had made mistakes but projected a positive approach as she declared:

Never say that you can't. You have to collaborate, you can't isolate yourself. You can't say, "Leave me alone because I've been teaching for many years and what I've done is good enough." Good enough is never enough! If you don't have high expectations for yourself, you can't expect your students to rise to the top either. You have to practice responsive teaching and identify student needs. You can't have blanket lessons. You must identify student strengths and weaknesses and work from there. Meet them where they are. A highly effective teacher will be supportive of their students' emotional as well as their academic needs. They all come into your classroom with different backgrounds and emotions. You have to embrace their disabilities and try to work towards solutions.

Ms. Logan emphasized the importance of establishing a "safe environment where students are comfortable to make mistakes and where they're encouraged to work towards correcting their mistakes." She described her classroom as one with "consistent rules and procedures, more student-centered learning versus teacher directed." Ms. Logan elaborated:

My classroom atmosphere is flexible and collaborative with cooperative learning. You have to have a good relationship with students and parents, even those that are difficult. I have a personality that smoothes things over.

When asked about how her students might describe a highly effective teacher, Ms. Logan said, "I think that they want their teacher to really get to know them and to treat them like a person, not just a number in their class." She elaborated:

> I think that a student appreciates when the teacher really knows who they are and not just their name. I think that's very significant because it makes them feel important. I think that they want a teacher who listens to them. They want their teacher to lead by example and be a mentor. They want their teacher to ensure that the learning environment is consistent, inviting and safe. They want their teacher to be accepting of diversity and uniqueness. They need teachers who will meet their emotional needs first because if you don't meet their emotional needs, you're going to lose them academically.

Knowledge, Experiences, and Factors

When asked about factors that have contributed most to her development as a highly effective teacher, Ms. Logan passionately proclaimed, "From day one, since 1997, I've always been a reflective person." She continued, "I think I'm a perfectionist and that's just something that I can't change nor do I want to although it makes me crazy sometimes." Ms. Logan expounded:

> If I can keep my expectations high for myself then it's going to positively affect the people around me. The proactive approach to self-study and professional development is key. I believe that teaching is a calling, a civic duty. My faith and my belief that teaching is a calling and this is what I'm supposed to do. I'm a Christian and I

think that I've been called to do this and I have to fulfill that calling. It's my way to serve the Lord.

When asked about significant events that have contributed to her teaching success, Ms. Logan recalled after an elongated pause:

I think that the biggest event was actually the two big times that I experienced failure professionally. One time was my second year. I quit teaching. I hated it and never wanted to do it again, ever. I had a bad experience, really bad, and I just quit. My mom said, "You have got to do something. We cannot stand you. You need to do something." I cried every day because I wasn't perfect at it. With hindsight, I wasn't good at it in my own mind.

So, I quit and went into something else. I was not fulfilled in the job I was doing. It was in an office and I liked the people I worked with, but it wasn't fulfilling. Then, I got called back into teaching. A principal at another school found an old resume' in a drawer and she called me out of nowhere and I said, "If it's meant to be, it's meant to be." So, I got back into education. I think that's a major reason for my striving towards highly effectiveness and to constantly seek professional development. I failed and I had to fix it.

Then, when I first moved to fourth grade, that first year was horrible. I failed tremendously. One third of the class failed the LEAP test that year and I felt responsible. I knew I wanted to succeed, but didn't know how. I didn't have all the tools, strategies, and trainings. One of my coworkers was fresh out of college and was lost, but was gifted. Her mind was always moving and she inspired me to start reading articles on best practices, how to teach reading comprehension, and what all these things meant. She was a huge inspiration and because of her, I read *Strategies That Work* by Stephanie Harvey and Anne Goudvis and reading and writing books by Kelly Gallagher.

Ms. Logan declared that she has embraced Compass, Louisiana's new teacher evaluation program. She reasoned, "Having those standards in front of me, because I'm goal oriented, I saw that, ok, well, how am I going to perfect this?" She continued, "So I had to change my ways to reflect the compass rubric." Ms. Logan concluded this section by describing the graduate classes in which she is currently enrolled as, "I have learned something out of every single class I've taken there."

When asked about which individuals have contributed to her development as a highly effective teacher, Ms. Logan immediately responded with the name of a current teaching colleague. She explained:

> We were in this together. She came to me for advice and I didn't know what to do and didn't have anything for her other than to help her in teaching writing, because it's an innate thing for me. She was the one that said, "Hey, I read this book. Why don't you read this book?" So she inspired

me to read those books and we started talking about the
books. We'd ask each other, "Did you try this, or that?"

Ms. Logan recalled that she has "taught with a lot of people
through the years because I've bounced around a lot and I think
I've learned something from every single teacher, but one that
stands out was an old school teacher." She shared about that early
experience:

> She taught me how to read test scores and to work from
> student strengths and weaknesses and how to work towards
> improving by meeting them where they were. Before the
> value-added model, when I first started, it [school
> performance score] was about how many students scored
> proficient. Before VAM [value-added model], I already
> worked under the understanding that I have to get every kid
> to grow academically. I think it was my old teacher friend
> who helped me to see how to do that.

Practices and Methods

When asked about preparing high quality and rigorous lesson
plans in terms of setting instructional outcomes, Ms. Logan
replied, "That is something that I've struggled with in the past,
because I'd become accustomed to teaching out of the textbook
that gives you the objectives." She further explained:

> When I stopped doing that [teaching out of the textbook] a
> couple years ago, I had a really hard time of making the
> perfect lesson plan. There were weeks that I didn't turn one
> in at all because I would get to class and I'd think, "Well I

know what I'm going to do today, but I don't know how to write it down and get it perfect." I always thought it was more of a technicality. I've found success not having it, but I feel that if I had the perfect lesson, I would be even more successful. So basically, I've winged it in the past.

I am taking a class on that [lesson planning] right now. The book is called, *Integrating Differentiated Instruction and Understanding by Design* by Tomlinson and McTighe. It teaches how to start from the big picture. You take the standard and then you work backwards from that. Before, I worked backwards from the LEAP test because I didn't know what else to do. I know that's not a good thing, but what else was I going to do? I didn't know! In the future, I will utilize backwards planning from common core standards and establish targeted goals and student friendly objectives. Then, I will generate several essential or guided questions as a map towards the outcome. I also want to integrate with my co-teachers to make sure that we have a cohesive unit.

When asked to describe her classroom management structure, Ms. Logan claimed that she was not a "natural born disciplinarian," but doesn't have significant discipline issues in her classroom. She has instituted a "democratic environment" in order to "teach students how to work cooperatively." She emphasized, "They need to be taught self-discipline." Ms. Logan discussed her behavior and consequences approach in greater detail:

They get a star on their punch card upon positive behavior and when it fills up, they get a tangible reward. Following negative behavior, they have silent lunch, which means they have to sit away from the other students. That is pretty effective. They don't want to do that. Another consequence for negative behavior is to sit out at recess.

When discussing classroom routines and procedures, Ms. Logan was quick to point out the importance of incorporating sustained silent reading into her daily lesson plan. She emphasized the significance of student writing and offered her opinion that, "Every teacher should be a teacher of literacy." She claimed, "I think on any standardized test, if a kid can write, they'll do well. When discussing her emphasis on sustained silent reading, she elucidated:

> I read a book by Donalyn Miller called *The Book Whisperer*. After reading that book, it became important to me to create a literacy environment. Teaching out of the textbook doesn't always allow for that so one of the things I did last year was to build in extended reading time at the beginning of class rather than as an afterthought or busy work. I started off with ten minutes of SSR [sustained silent reading] and then we extended it to 15 minutes, then 20 [minutes]. The students at first whined, but then after maybe two weeks, the timer would go off and they'd ask to finish their chapter. I'd hear them talk with their neighbors about this or that book and it started an intrinsic thing for

them.

You have to find ways to get them interested in what they're reading by exposing them to good literature. Textbooks limit you. If you let them explore things that they're interested in, they're going to do it. I allow them to pick out their own books. I've spent a lot of my own money trying to expand my classroom library. We go to the library twice a week and I encourage them to get at least one chapter book.

I have a lot of success using Accelerated Reader [reading software program] as a tracking device. The students select a goal based on their capability after taking the STAR test which gives us a baseline measurement and then tells them their range of proximal development. One of the mistakes I've made in the past was limiting what they read. If you limit them, they won't read magazines or articles on the internet so I now include a writing response component. They may take the [Accelerated Reader] test to keep track of their points but if they read something outside of AR, they'll get credit for that too.

In the past, I used SSR as a filler, but when I started putting it at the beginning of the class period, they became intrinsically motivated. Now, when they finish class work, they go back to their book without me telling them to. They just do it. They really want to read and I know the more kids read, the better they will perform on tests. I think that was the biggest contributor to their overall success.

Ms. Logan claimed that orchestrating high-level questioning and discussion is an area in which she uses a lot of partner talks. She prefers groups of two students rather than four "because they have more turns to participate." She credited scaffolding as a means of meeting students where they are and progressively moving them toward stronger understanding and greater independence in the learning process. Ms. Logan explained:

> We have less whole group and more targeted small group instruction. I asked more open ended questions. I tried to provide more authentic learning. I don't use workbooks or any of that. I used more authentic literature. I got rid of the textbook altogether as self-selected reading is important. They self-assessed and maintained their own records and goals. The students are very honest in keeping their records.
>
> In my classroom, you'll hear purposeful noise and a lot of good student discussion. I facilitate and encourage student generated questions and an easy way to do that is to make them read and teach them thinking stems...I notice, I think, I realize, I visualize, I wonder. When they read, they think of and write down these questions and that helps for them to have good, rich conversations with each other. The speaking, writing, and listening help students to become independent thinkers and learners. I make them speak in

complete sentences when they talk. If they explain it to each other, they'll understand it better, and it provides an authentic experience.

Ms. Logan summarized her questioning philosophy by declaring, "I ask a lot of open ended, higher order questions, and allow students to feed off of those conversations. I speak as minimally as possible."

When asked how she ensures that all students are engaged, Ms. Logan indicated that she has tried several different approaches including, "cute activities and games" that she deemed "unproductive." She expounded:

> I used to spend hours making games and cute centers. I don't think they're productive or effective so I don't use them anymore. For example, we were required to make all these centers to occupy the kids like a game on adjectives while we were working with a small group. That's just busy work. If you just have them read and write, they're going to learn more. It's going to expand their options everywhere else. I remember spending 30 dollars on games with colorful pages and folders. It was a total waste of time.

Her primary strategy for ensuring that all students are engaged is to promote and provide classroom opportunities for cooperative learning. She commented:

> One of the things I do is try to facilitate. I really want them to be self-disciplined and accountable, and I try to reinforce

that. I walk around the room, listen to what they say when they speak, and take notes. A lot of times, I use partner talk. I'll ask a question and instead of just a few people raising their hand, I'll say, "Ok. Talk to your partner about..." and then that makes everyone have to talk about it. Then, I'll say, "Ok who has an answer?" That way, everyone will then have something to say even though I may not call on them. They've all participated in the original question. I try to make sure that when I do call on one single person, I try to get everyone. The more they talk, if it's purposeful, the more they're involved and therefore the more they're learning.

In a discussion regarding assessment and monitoring student learning, Ms. Logan indicated that until recently enrolling in a graduate course, she had difficulty understanding the difference between summative and formative assessments. She explained:

I now understand the difference between summative and formative assessment. Some teachers don't fully understand it. I think not understanding the difference is a problem because some teachers think every test they give students is an end result and they need to take a grade on it. Some teachers don't go back and address the mistakes. In that case, there's no corrective feedback. It just gets graded and then move on. That's not good for the students.

Ms. Logan expressed minor frustration with the requirement of a minimum number of graded assignments per grading period. She commented:

> We have to have nine grades per nine weeks, so I have to
> give weekly tests. I don't always like that but I have to.
> Therefore, we'll do weekly spelling tests or I'll give some
> type of quiz on whatever it is in reading that were doing or
> in English so that I make sure to get enough grades. But
> the authentic things like their class work, their thinking
> sheets and things like that, I give points for because I think
> it's valuable. I collect all of their work and see their
> responses and give them a variety of points.

Ms. Logan shared that "conferencing is one of the things that I
do now that I didn't realize before was a best practice." She
elaborated and provided an example:

> When I teach writing, I didn't know how else to do this but
> I'd call the kids up one at a time to go over what they
> wrote. I would give them corrective feedback. This is how
> you fix this or that. That's a very effective way. I didn't
> know that was so effective until hindsight. An example is
> that a summative assessment wasn't working because all of
> the years I taught 4th grade, I'd always give them a written
> response question, one per week, because I feel like quality
> over quantity is better. It didn't always have to have
> evidence from the passage, but I did include that when it
> became a component. What I would get when I first started
> teaching was a one sentence answer and I wouldn't let them
> go back and fix it. I now allow them to go back. I'll say,

"This is not enough. I need you to tell me more. Can you go back and reread this part?" and only until they meet my standards, can they then turn in the test. I thought I was wrong for that. Like I'm cheating, but now I realize I'm just giving them corrective feedback. They'll never give me what I'm asking them to do if I don't show them.

Ms. Logan concluded our discussion on this section by stating, "I use formative assessment to drive instruction."

Support Systems

When asked how her administrator(s) prepared her for the Compass observations, Ms. Logan replied, "They gave us a copy of the compass rubric ahead of time to look at and study. I started using that as a guide to prepare myself for my observation." When reflecting on the observation experience, Ms. Logan explained:

We didn't have a pre-conference for the second one, but for the first one, I was able to type up exactly what she should look for. They gave us the opportunity to point out something I or the students did that they may not have seen. They allowed us to come in and justify that we did meet a component. Because we were allowed to turn the pre-observation answers in written form, I was able to clearly articulate what the observer(s) would see before the lesson. That way, they could look for those things in particular. I was able to frontload the observer with what I was going to do. In case they missed something while I taught, they would have that to go back on and jog their memory. The post observation conferences were face-to-face and that was beneficial to hear someone else's perspective. I could see where I need to work from and improve.

Ms. Logan recalled several different professional development opportunities in which she has participated that have led to her highly effective rating. She cited Kagan training as well as a workshop in which the Common Core State Standards were "unpacked." Regarding the standards unpacking workshop, she noted, "It helped to identify what the actual standard means and how to take the verbs from it and work backwards from there." After reading books about it, Ms. Logan petitioned her district for Kagan training. She claimed, "I had been using it but I was just going by the book that I bought and I kept asking, 'Can we please get this training?'" She said, "I think our teachers can benefit. They don't know how to shift from being teacher directed to student centered." It took about two years, but last summer we got trained.

Ms. Logan also mentioned a conference she attended a couple summers ago at which she learned about "how to teach every student like they're gifted." She followed with, "That was probably one of the first things that sparked me to want to change and do things differently than the way I was doing it before."

Upon reflecting on what she needed from local and state levels of education in order to maintain highly effectiveness, Ms. Logan declared:

From the school level, I need continued support and open

lines of communication. Our people are pretty good and very supportive at the school level. I think they do a good job of supporting us. On the district level, I would like for them to respect and value my contributions and dedication to this parish. I would like for them to listen. I would like for them to view me as an asset or resource and not as a threat. I'd like for them to provide more relevant training for everyone. At the state level, they need to continue updating their website. They should implement new things in a realistic time frame, accept input from real educators, and to provide more relevant trainings.

Ms. Logan concluded by offering, "I don't want my name on the billboard, but it would be nice to simply have someone say thank you for your dedication. I'd like for them to value my input but I'm not doing this for them, I'm doing it for my students."

10. MS. TURNER

Ms. Turner has been in education for nine years. She currently teaches seventh grade American History with previous classroom experiences in sixth grade World History and seventh grade Reading. She obtained her bachelor's degree from a regional university in southwest Louisiana. She is certified to teach social studies in kindergarten through eighth grades. The school at which she taught during the 2013-2014 school year is located in an urban area where 46% of the student population qualified for free or reduced lunch. Ms. Turner cited childhood struggles with dyslexia and an early death of her father as challenges that have strengthened her ability to empathize with at-risk students. She credited her experiences in a non-education workforce and being a military wife for her work ethic and flexibility. She has gone above and beyond her job description by organizing student trips to Washington D.C. and New York.

Definition of Highly Effective Teaching

When asked to describe what highly effective teaching meant to her, Ms. Turner quickly replied, "It's simple, just doing my job."

She qualified her answer by further stating, "They told me what I needed to do and I did it, but I did it my way." Ms. Turner commented, "I see things in a strategic way." She compared her job to that of a football coach and elucidated:

> I see iLEAP [state standardized assessment] as the Super bowl and I get my team ready to win. I have tricks up my sleeve to get us there. I condition them all year long for the Super Bowl. First, you have to have classroom discipline. I had the honor of hearing a man named Mark McLeod a few years ago at a middle school conference. He spoke my language.
>
> I don't have classroom rules. We have procedures and it's all based on respect. I respect you. You respect me. I add into their emotional bank account so that when I do take a withdrawal, I'm not on negative so they don't shut me down. I tell a lot of stories of myself when I was their age and about my kids so I make it personal in here. That way, they buy into what I'm selling. Just like in football practice, it's a lot of repetitive work. We study together so I can ensure that they understand and build a foundation and then add to the foundation by going more in depth with the material.

Ms. Turner recommended that a highly effective teacher "must have passion and compassion." She explained, "You have to have passion for what you teach and compassion for the kids." She provided the following examples:

The way you present the information has to be fun because you're dealing with a techie generation. I'm not techie, but I may stand on a desk. I act things out. I dress up in costume. We have fun. You can't assign busy work. They can sniff that out. So anytime I assign something, rarely do I hear, "Is this for a grade?" They know everything I give out is important. I don't waste their time because I don't' like my time wasted. They know everything is important.

It's also important to connect the information to an emotion so they remember it. Review, review, review. Competition. I always use other schools as our competition. I use the other school's test scores as a form of motivation. Kids love to win, so I use competition to my advantage.

When asked how her students may describe her, Ms. Turner stated, "A teacher who hasn't forgotten what it's like to be a student." She included, "Organized, knowledgeable of content, nice, helpful, and understanding." She expounded on her rapport with her students:

I allow do-overs. I correct things and give it back to them so that can make an A. I set them up for success and not failure. If they keep making bad grades, they'll think they can't do it and shut down. I'll take the time to redo things or guide them to the correct answer. I allow them to come to class before school. I'll stay at lunch if they need me and I'll stay after school if they need it. So, they're able to get that one on one. If they feel like, "I'm smart", then they'll give it their all.   They like privileges. I allow them to eat and drink in my class as a reward as long as they behave. I told one student that he needed to come to school more often. I made a deal with him. I said if he came to school for an entire six weeks period, I'll buy donuts for the class. He came to school because of the peer pressure. Everyone wanted their donuts. After he did it, he noticed that his grades went up. I said, "Well, there you go bubba. It's because you're doing your work and coming to school every day."

Knowledge, Experiences, and Factors

When asked about factors that have contributed most to her development as a highly effective teacher, Ms. Turner credited, "Being a struggling student as a child." She described her childhood challenges:

> I have dyslexia and no one understood what that was back then. I always had to struggle for my grades, so I know the frustration of being a struggling learner. We had the perfect family until my Dad died when I was 11 and then my mother became an alcoholic. By middle school, my sister and I took care of getting ourselves to school. We made sure to keep our grades up because I cheered and she was an athlete. I understand what it's like to have an absent parent and a deceased parent.

Ms. Turner then spoke about her pre-teacher experiences. She noted that because she started teaching at a later age than the average teacher, she hasn't "burned out." She commented:

> I began teaching at an older age. I was 31 when I began. I was in the workforce where I developed a work ethic. My husband was in the military, so we moved around a lot. It helped that I was older when I started teaching. I don't think I would have done this job in my early 20s the way I'm doing it now. I think I would have been burned out and would not have been this caliber of a teacher had I started in my early 20s. I've had very good mentors. When I was a student teacher, the lady I student taught under taught me a lot. She was a nurturer but wasn't one of those sugary kind. You knew she loved you but was strict and I liked that.

When asked to discuss individuals and events that contributed to her development as a highly effective teacher, Ms. Turner reflected on the positive impact and influences of her past and current school administrators as well as her teaching colleagues. She disclosed:

> At both schools I've taught, the administration was phenomenal. They know I take care of business in my classroom so any time I need something, they're willing to help. Last year, I asked my principal if the school could help me bring students to Washington DC. They let me go on these little trips and help with footing the bill. My principals "get" me. If you look at the rubric, I'm nothing

like the rubric. My principal tells others who ask how I'm so successful, "She's old school." She doesn't do all of the new strategies. She does her own thing. They let me go rogue, they don't ask questions as long as I'm getting my job done. I appreciate that. They don't micromanage me. They make my life easy so I can do my crazy stuff. When I'm walking down the hall wearing a continental uniform and a gun, they just let me go. I'm blessed that I've been surrounded with good, positive people at the schools I've worked at. I work with a group of girls on my team...when the old principal combined our team, he knew what he was doing. I consider us to be the A-Team and they're my best friends. During the week of testing, after the kids get finished with a test and we go to classes, these broads are doing PowerPoints [presentation software] in history for me. Whichever subject is next, we review with the students, we help each other out. For testing, we make sure we're up. We don't let anyone get lazy. The kids understand that this is important and they can't just blow it off. It's a true team. It's a team effort. I'm like Patton. I rally the troops. I give the speech. It's nothing for us to sing down the hall and the kids think it's cool to be on our team. Now, we're not their friends. We get the job done, but we're here to have fun too.

Ms. Turner has taken several educational trips to various American history-laden locations. She cited those trips as significant experiences in her quest to become even more knowledgeable of her course content. She described:

> I took a class offered by the Louisiana endowment of the humanities in which you get college credit. At the end of the semester, they chose two people to go to DC. That trip was the only reason I took the class because I'd always wanted to go to DC. I won it and I've gone back and haven't paid for a trip yet. That's where I learn my stuff. I go to Williamsburg. I take kids. We do the educational tours.   Last year, we went to New York. I had 36 kids with me. It always makes me so proud because people there are always impressed with their knowledge and how well behaved they are. That keeps my fire going because I get to learn and see it through their eyes. That's where I get and keep that little fire burning.

Ms. Turner also mentioned her students and former teachers as those who have contributed to her highly effective rating. She elaborated:

> Students, I always want to make a difference with them. When I get that connection with a kid who walks in here saying I hate history, I start with the revolution and they just buy into it. Some of my former teachers have impacted my life. I've been blessed to have really good people and teachers in my life. I'm still in touch with some of my elementary school teachers.

Practices and Methods

When asked about preparing high quality and rigorous lesson plans in terms of setting instructional outcomes, Ms. Turner explained:

> I print the test out first. That way, it keeps me on track. From there, I have a whole unit where it's everything they need to know. We go over it, I post the answers on the wall. That way, we can rock n roll. It's backwards design, but again, if you want a formal lesson plan, you're not going to get it. In my head, there's a method to the madness. It's not a formal lesson plan where it says I'll say this, "The students' will do this..." For formal observations, I just go to one of my team teachers and she makes it pretty for me. You can have the prettiest lesson plan on earth and be the worst teacher ever.

When discussing her classroom management procedures and routines, Ms. Turner mentioned the significance of taking advantage of every instructional minute from bell to bell. She noted:

> When they walk in, they know exactly what's going to take place. I have the page on the board, what they need to turn in, and a reminder to sharpen your pencil. We walk in as a class, so they know to take care of things quickly before we get going. Sometimes I assign jobs to students, such as to tell students what they need to do when they're absent. Sometimes I'll do a warm-up, but to me bell ringers take up

too much instructional time unless we're reviewing for the
iLEAP.   It's expectations; they know what's going to
happen. Daily routines, same thing happens every day.
My classroom may be rearranged, but I never have my
desks in rows. They're always facing different ways,
because I like to have the stage. By this time, the kids
know what to do and will redirect each other. At the end of
the class, we recap the day's lesson.

When asked how she orchestrates high-level questioning and
discussion in the classroom, Ms. Turner claimed that she
incorporates a scaffolding technique. Ms. Turner described:

I know who can answer the hard questions so I'll start with
the easy ones so everyone is successful in my class. I set
the foundation, then I can scaffold the questions and ask
harder questions or use different verbiage. I tell them to
give me a 7th grade answer when they answer me. I use
rapid fire questioning to get all of them involved in the
discussion. I use "why" a lot to get them to dig deeper into
the content.

Ms. Turner summarized her questioning philosophy by declaring,
"I'm a control freak and so group work drives me nuts. It's hard for
me to let go and that's bad on my part because I am a control freak
so I'm in control of the questioning."

When asked how she ensures that all students are engaged,
Ms. Turner promptly replied, "If you'd ask my kids, I think it's
because I love what I teach and they can see the passion in what I

teach. It's hard not to pay attention." She elaborated:

> I think I scare some kids because I get excited. I get in their face. I stand on things. One day my principal walked by and I was standing on a desk teaching. He looked in and said, "Never mind," and walked out. It's passion. Make those kids who are hard to love, make them buy into what you're selling like the kid who doesn't like coming to school. When a student drifts off, I just go stand next to him, the proximity thing. If it's a problem, I give you one bad day, but if it's an ongoing problem, I have a come to Jesus meeting outside in the hallway and tell them, "Help me help you." Usually, I'll find out that maybe they're being picked on or something else. I tell them, "When you're ready to act like a seventh grader, you're more than welcome to rejoin my class."

In a discussion regarding assessment and monitoring student learning, Ms. Turner started by describing her formative assessment strategies. She commented:

> I don't' have activotes [electronic response system], so they fold paper into four sections. I'll ask a question. It'll be multiple choice. They close their eyes before giving me the answer. That's just for me to see if they got it and we can move on. There's different things in the toolbox to see if they get it or not. I use a lot of questioning. If I see they don't have it, I go back and re-teach.

Ms. Turner then proceeded to explain her summative

assessment methods with an emphasis on the importance of using a format similar to that of the state standardized test. She described in more detail:

> Each chapter of the book has four sections. With each section, I'll use the reproducible if it's good. I'll have a vocabulary test and then an iLEAP [state standardized test] style test at the end of the unit. I don't want busy work. An iLEAP style test is one in which there are both multiple choice and about four questions to answer but they choose two open-ended or constructed response questions. That way, when they do get to the real iLEAP, they're familiar with the format.

> On test day, I'll go over a few things before the test. On the day before, we take the whole class period and study together using jeopardy games and such. They know exactly what's going to be on the test. I don't have any surprises. I'll walk around and when I see they're finishing, I'll go back to my desk. They'll come up to me and I'll glance real quick and mark the ones they got wrong, hand it back to them. They go back to their seats correct it, and turn it in. They're not able to use their notes, but this process gets them to rethink their wrong answer. With computers, I can now upload my tests so it's read to those students who need the test read aloud to meet their IEP requirements.

Support Systems

When asked how her administrator(s) prepared her for the Compass observations, Ms. Turner indicated that her administrators helped to put her at ease. She recalled:

> They just told me to do what I do best. I put more stress on myself than they do. They tell me what the rubric needs and they explain to me everything that the rubric says, what they have to look for. They somehow plug it in. I'm not a cookie cutter teacher. I think outside the box. I'm comfortable with it. The kids are comfortable with it. If they don't buy into it, I'll come up with something else to sell, but right now it's working for me. I love that they took the stress off.

Reflecting on the observation experience, Ms. Turner said, "They make me think, how can I do it better?" She further acknowledged the support she received from her administrators:

> Things that I don't see that they see, help me to get better. The principal gave me an idea on how to make sure that all students are actively engaged by just asking the question, "How am I sure that all are involved?" They make me feel good about myself. They're my cheerleaders. Anything they want me to change or do, I'll do because they support me.

Ms. Turner claimed that of all of the professional development opportunities in which she has participated, "the field trips to Washington DC and New York" have been the most valuable. She expressed that she takes the initiative to explore instructional strategies and content ideas. She illustrated:

> I do a lot of research online. I go to other parishes to see what they're doing. Last summer, I saw which parishes outscored me and I went to their websites to see what their teachers had on their websites for their kids to use. I go to Texas school websites to see what they're doing. I find treasures online that help me. Through independent research, I find a lot of really good things on other district websites.

Reflecting on what she needed from local and state levels of education in order to maintain highly effectiveness, Ms. Turner expressed a need for additional funding for content-related field trips. She added that she'd like to see more meaningful and relevant "professional development workshops and classroom resources." She concluded by offering, "The district and state should be giving us more resources instead of me having to find my own."

11. MS. DAVID

Ms. David has been a classroom teacher for five years. She currently teaches seventh grade math. Prior to her recent classroom assignment, she taught in both a self-contained classroom as well as an inclusion special education setting. She obtained her bachelor's degree in social work from a regional university in northwest Louisiana. She is 12 hours away from obtaining a master's degree at a university in central Louisiana. She is certified to teach math in grades five through nine. The school at which she taught during the 2013-2014 school year is situated in a rural area where 40% of the student population qualified for free or reduced lunch. While she has only been in the teaching profession for a relatively short period of time, Ms. David has the demeanor of a seasoned veteran when discussing classroom management and instructional practices.

Definition of Highly Effective Teaching

Ms. David defined highly effective teaching as "teaching with a specific purpose every day." She added, "Never just showing up and doing whatever flies out of your head." She claimed that the characteristics of a highly effective teacher include, "a lot of energy, motivation, and a good rapport with students." She emphasized the importance of using instructional time wisely with, "I teach from bell to bell. When the first bell rings or even before the first bell rings, they know not to be late." She added, "We have a warm up on the board. They get started with that and then we're working for two hours. We teach. We learn. We talk. It's always with a purpose." Ms. David further described her emphasis on using classroom time efficiently:

> I think the bell to bell teaching is something we all do here and is highly encouraged. No wasted time. You don't just let half the class take it easy and talk because the other half just left to go to a ballgame, which happens a lot in a small school like this. We still continue on.

Commenting on how she manages her class time, Ms. David added, "Students know the rules up front. We spend a lot of time in the first few weeks going over procedures and routines. By the fourth week, if a kid does something not in procedure, the other kids correct him or her."

Ms. David cited her degree in social work as a positive factor in developing a cooperative and productive rapport with her students. She illustrated:

> Good student rapport is extremely important because kids have to be motivated too and if you offend them or if they feel like they have to be defensive, then they won't perform well on a day-to-day basis. My degree is in social work so

I've learned some people skills. My goal is not necessarily to be the nice teacher. I have plenty of friends outside of school. I tell them, "I'm not here to be your friend, but hey, if by the end of the year we're friends, that's good." Of course, there's some that I have personality conflicts with, but for the most part, I think they'll say that they love my class. I'm strict but they like it. My students would also say that I smile a lot even when I try to be stern. I'm always willing to help. I don't ever mind working with them during lunch or after school.

Knowledge, Experiences, and Factors

When asked about factors that have contributed most to her development as a highly effective teacher, Ms. David credited her experiences in special education. She expounded:

I had to learn about different learning styles and ways to differentiate and that really helped me to be a regular classroom teacher. If I would have just jumped into the regular classroom, I wouldn't have related so much to different learners, not just slower learners, but also gifted students. I know how to modify assignments to keep everyone involved and learning. Knowing what an IEP is, how it's developed, being able to read, and understand those documents has been a big help.

When asked about significant events that have contributed to her teaching success, Ms. David pointed out that the school has had significant administrative changes in the past few years. She noted that through the changes in administrative philosophies, she's become more flexible and adaptive. With a positive approach, she noted, "I've learned to change everything all the time, however they need it. In the process, I've learned what I like to do." She's also met the changes in state standards with a willingness to do what it takes to benefit her students.

Despite being relatively new to the teaching profession, she was selected to represent her school at state-level meetings as a "teacher leader." Ms. David noted, "I'm the teacher leader for our school so I go to all the meetings about curriculum. I feel like I understand the standards and I'm more prepared to communicate with fellow teachers about them now from all of these meetings and conferences."

Ms. David attended a National Council for Teachers in Math conference at which she learned a lot about how to incorporate tactile learning. Regarding the NCTM conference, she stated, "I've learned more from that conference than any others."

Ms. David referred to all of her past teachers and professors when asked about which individuals have contributed to her development as a highly effective teacher. Ms. David indicated she's learned much about "what they do that I like and don't like."

Practices and Methods

When asked about preparing high quality and rigorous lesson plans setting instructional outcomes, Ms. David replied, "Whenever I know I'm going to be observed, I spend weeks designing a lesson whereas truth be known, I don't do that on a daily basis." She added, "It makes me sound brilliant, but I'm not, I'm just a regular teacher." She continued:

> I'll try to find something online that's been vetted that goes along with my textbook because we weren't' given anything other than websites to look at. Until I get a new textbook, I've decided I'm going to use mine, add to it, and enhance it with HOT [higher order thinking] questions, group activity, hands on, etc.
>
> The textbook has definitely been a help this year to get us through what was supposed to be a transitional year. I make sure I include everything. I do warm up, teacher activity, student activity, list all math practices, accelerated math [software program]. I plan formally about a week in advance, but I have the course informally planned out to the end of the year on the calendar. It's not fancy. I know exactly what we're going to do up until the last day of school.

When Ms. David discussed her routines and procedures regarding classroom management, she reiterated her emphasis on maximizing instructional classroom time. She elucidated:

> They have warm up right when they come in the door. I give them about five minutes and right now it's consisting of the new iLEAP practice test assessment items a page a day, about three questions on the page. Then, I choose a random student. They love to go to the board and play teacher. They facilitate the discussion of the questions.

They don't just go up there and solve it, they have to use HOT [higher order thinking] questions and get that discussion going. Then, we talk about our purpose statement of what we're going to do today. Afterwards, we go into the lesson. I facilitate the notes.

I think it's important that they do see an example of modeling first. I go over a new assignment or new lesson and then after about 25-30 minutes of discussing and practicing it, they're given an assignment. Sometimes it's independent work designed to last about 15 minutes. Sometimes it's group work. If it's independent, we always have a partner check the next day. After the lesson, they start their independent mode. Even if it's group work, they go into their accelerated math [software program]. It's all individualized.

Ms. David claimed that orchestrating high-level questioning and discussion is an area in which she encourages a student-led process. She invests time at the beginning of the school year modeling meaningful questioning with expectations that her students will eventually lead that process. After a student leads the questioning and discussion activity, they'll review and critique the session. She noted, "It's positive. We don't criticize."

When asked about student engagement, Ms. David acknowledged she ensures all students are engaged. She stated, "I think with junior high, it's hard to keep them all engaged. However, I've learned if I'm moving and I'm around the room, I'm much more capable of interjecting than if I'm just sitting here at my desk." She added, "I never sit. A professor of mine said, 'A teacher on her feet is worth three on their seat'. That's why when I get home from work, I'm exhausted!"

In a discussion regarding assessment and monitoring student learning, Ms. David was quick to point out that her students have said that she's "the fastest teacher at getting our grades back to us." She expounded:

> I grade all tests that night. They get it back the next day and talk about it as soon as they come in. I think immediate feedback is very important because they can still remember what they were thinking when they put that answer. If you wait too long, they don't remember why or how they put the wrong answer.

Regarding how she constructs and grades her summative assessments, Ms. David said, "I use some questions from the textbook and I'll use some from the practice iLEAP tests even if it doesn't relate to the topic we're learning at that time." She continued:

> They know that those practice questions can be in there at any time. I'll pull some activities from the internet and ask specific questions from those activities. I try for the tests to not be too lengthy. I feel like they're challenged, but I should say that my average is usually about 90%. I think that's because they get a very similar quiz, a little smaller, maybe 20 questions the day before. We go over it right

before the test and then they get a 50 question test. If I had a lot of kids not do well, we'd have a retest, but that doesn't happen very often at all.

Support Systems

When asked about how her administrator(s) prepared her for the Compass observations, Ms. David stated that she was already familiar with the Danielson rubric from some of her recent college courses. She also offered that her former principal was "laid back." According to Ms. David, the principal said, "Here's what I'm going to be looking for. Make sure you cover all of this." Ms. David added, "There was a set of questions that was emailed to me and I just filled it in and sent them back, but other than that, we didn't talk a lot about it." She reflected on the observation and post-observation conference process:

> I think it helped me to see where I need to grow. Some of my questions weren't as high order and critical thinking as they needed to be. I realized that was something I had to work on. Being able to talk about it right after was beneficial.

When asked what types of professional development activities have been most beneficial in preparing her for highly effective teaching, Ms. David cited, without hesitation, her pedagogical experiences at Louisiana College.

Upon reflecting on what she needed from local and state levels of education in order to maintain highly effectiveness, Ms. David acknowledged a need for "updated materials, textbooks, and technology." She stated:

> It's ridiculous to have us go to websites that may or may not be vetted. When we do that, we're supposed to present it to our curriculum supervisor before we can present it to our kids and sometimes that takes a long time. As a parent, I don't want someone who has never been part of a curriculum team to design my son's curriculum. People who are paid to do that and are very good at it should be doing it.

12. Ms. Flynn

Ms. Flynn has been a fifth grade teacher for all of her nine years in education. For the last eight years, she has taught all subjects (ELA, Math, Science, Social Studies) with six different lesson plans per day. This year, she is teaching fifth grade math exclusively.

Ms. Flynn obtained her bachelor's degree from a regional university in south Louisiana. She is certified to teach grades first through fifth. The school at which she taught during the 2013-2014 school year is located in an urban area where 79% of the student population qualified for free or reduced lunch. She expressed great pride in having a deep understanding of the content standards as well as facilitating a classroom that is fun, yet very well structured.

Definition of Highly Effective Teaching

Ms. Flynn defined highly effective teaching as planning for "100% student success." She reasoned, "You won't always reach 100% but then that's where you go back in and modify your plans, re-teach, so that you can try to get as close to 100% success rate as possible." She added, "Highly effective teaching should include differentiation, scaffolding, introducing your skill at the appropriate lowest level and building it up." Ms. Flynn emphasized the importance of caring as "one of the top characteristics." She also included, "Being funny, having high expectations of yourself and your students." She further advised, "You must have routines in place, a constant learning environment in which you're spiraling your activities with a deep understanding of the standards, knowing where your students need to be at the end of the year."

When Ms. Flynn was asked what she thought might be the definition of a highly effective teacher from a student's perspective, she replied:

> A teacher who never gives up on them who has a loving and caring attitude towards them so that they know that he or she truly cares if they're successful. One who rewards them for positive behavior and gives them encouraging feedback. A teacher who dances and sings, uses a lot of hand gestures to help them remember things. A teacher who is fun so that the students enjoy coming to your classroom. Most of all, one who is caring...they can sense that.

Knowledge, Experiences, and Factors

When asked about factors that have contributed most to her development as a highly effective teacher, Ms. Flynn credited, "Professional developments workshops, Pinterest [social network sharing website], my coworkers and high expectations from my principal." She continued, "I'm constantly looking on the internet doing personal research. A lot of highly effective teachers probably post a lot on Pinterest. I don't post much, but I sure do steal from them." She also mentioned, "Having genuine concern for my students that I get them where they need to be." When asked about significant events that have contributed to her teaching success, Ms. Flynn recalled:

> I attended the Center for Development and Learning in
> New Orleans where there were different workshops. I went
> to a Mark Diamond workshop in which he taught us how to
> teach students to write narratives that I found very
> beneficial in my classroom.

Practices and Methods

When asked about preparing high quality and rigorous lesson plans in terms of setting instructional outcomes, Ms. Flynn replied, "I like to do that backwards in which you make the test first by looking at the standards, what the students need to know, and then teach them to be successful in meeting those standards." She expounded:

> We're following Engage New York [curriculum]. I like it
> because of the way the lessons are designed. They start off
> very hands on, very visual; and then they move to paper
> and pencil. The first questions are, "Here's the problem.
> Work it," and then it moves into word problems where the
> last word problem is very high level. I start with the end in

mind. What is my test going to look like? What do my students need to know based on the standards and how will I teach them to be successful on the test?

When I asked Ms. Flynn to describe her daily classroom routine, she confidently stated, "When they come in, they know to unpack, get out their homework from the night before, and there's always a bell ringer on the board. They know exactly what to do."

Ms. Flynn protects instructional time by using signals or gestures to nonverbally communicate with students and checks homework while students are working on the bell-ringer. She explained:

> We go over their homework and look at the answers. If they need help, then I go over the ones they had problems with. If they need to go to the restroom or have a question, instead of raising their hand and interrupting the class, we have a little signal or gesture for each situation. I can just acknowledge nonverbally and keep teaching without interruption. For example, if they need their pencil sharpened, they just point to the tip. I have many efficiency processes in order to maximize instructional time. There's little stopping. I know what they need, they do it and we continue learning.
>
> When I want the whole class to answer, I have a specific gesture. If I want a single person to answer, there's a gesture (raise hand). I do a lot of think-pair-share in which I'll read something to them and then say, "Think about it.

Don't say anything yet. Just think about your answer," because some get it right away, but some need a little more time to think about their answer. Then, I'll ask them to get with their partner so those who need a little help can discuss it with their partner when they share. It gives those students who struggle a little bit of a chance to participate because their partner just told them and now they feel successful. I don't have many discipline problems at all. To prevent negative behavior, students are constantly engaged. They don't have time to misbehave. From the time they walk in to the time they pack up, there's something to do.

Ms. Flynn concluded this section by indicating that she incorporates a strategy that students can use to organize and identify information as they read a passage or word problem.

When asked to describe how she orchestrates high-level questioning and discussion Ms. Flynn stated, "I give them question starters that help them start their questioning such as, 'Why do you think...'?" She illustrated:

Sometimes they're just working together in centers or working in their binders. I'll tell them, "Don't just tell them the answer, you need to show them how we did it." I'll give them examples. I'll say, "I'm your partner, these are the things you should be telling your partner." I show them how to talk to and question each other based on my modeling. I invest time at the beginning of the school year modeling how they should question each other.

Ms. Flynn commented that she ensures that all students are engaged by using a nonverbal strategies to constantly check for understanding and focus. She elaborated:

> I use a lot of hands on, visual activities and constantly checking with them with fist to five [fist means no understanding, five indicates full understanding] to ensure they're engaged at all times. Sometimes with a multiple choice situation, I'll have them form the answer with sign language to show me they understand and are engaged. I can do a real quick check for understanding and engagement. Using white boards, they write down their answer and show it to me all at one time. When reading a problem, I may stop at a word and they'll have to fill it in. I use lots of little strategies to keep them constantly engaged and following along. If they drift off or become a little distracting, I walk nearby, or give them the look.

Ms. Flynn uses an exit ticket as means of formatively monitoring student learning. She noted, "Once they learn the lesson, they fill out the exit ticket and I check off whether they got everything right or if there's something they missed." She then described her summative assessment method:

> We have a test every Friday. In my centers system, I have a teacher center so I can go back to visit with each of them on the standards they're having problems with. Most of my tests in math are mostly word problems with some multiple

choice and some open ended questions. I try to have a good mixture. I'll have them draw a picture and explain to me how they got to the answer. If they fail the test, sometimes I allow them to come in from recess and retake it. Usually, I'm able to do that in my teacher center as part of the center's process.

Support Systems

When asked about how her administrator(s) prepared her for the Compass observations, Ms. Flynn replied, "We had a pre-observation conference in which we looked at the lesson plans, the rubric and what she'll be looking for during the observation." She added, "We have that time to talk about some unique situations in terms of students who have special needs or requirements."

Reflecting on the benefits of the observation experience, Ms. Flynn recalled, "She was able to point some things out that I didn't see." She continued, "While I'm teaching next time, I'll be aware of those things. It was great feedback on what I'm doing right as well as what I need to improve on."

When asked what she needed from local and state levels of education in order to maintain highly effectiveness, Ms. Flynn quickly mentioned, "ongoing professional development." After a few moments of reflection, she added, "materials, resources, textbooks, and manipulatives."

13. MS. MANNING

Ms. Manning has been in education for 12 years. Prior to teaching fifth grade math for the last seven years, she taught high school special education. She is currently employed as an instructional coach at an elementary school. She obtained her bachelor's and master's degrees from a regional university in southwest Louisiana. She is certified to teach regular education, grades first through eighth. She is also certified in special education, grades kindergarten through twelfth. The school at which she taught during the 2013-2014 school year is located in a suburban area where 55% of the student population qualified for free or reduced lunch. Ms. Manning cited a former principal and her father, a former teacher, as being the main contributors to her highly effective rating. Her former principal provided numerous meaningful professional development opportunities while her father was the source of her inspiration to enter the education profession.

Definition of Highly Effective Teaching

Ms. Manning defined highly effective teaching as "a classroom in which students are highly engaged, using questioning techniques, leading each other towards discovery of the content or concept." Ms. Manning described a highly effective teacher as one who has a "good personality." She advised, "You need to have a well-rounded personality with a lot of energy. Yet, you also need to have patience to sit back and allow your students to take control of your classroom."

Ms. Manning listed "caring and compassion for kids" when describing her characteristics as a highly effective teacher. She elaborated:

> I think that kids are willing to work for me because they like me and can tell that I like them and am here for them. In terms of behavior, I think a highly effective teacher displays compassion for children and the kids respect that. When you walk into my classroom, you'll see students at work. I will be either flowing through the students or I'll be pulling students for differentiated instruction. I do believe that not all students are at the same level. Differentiated instruction and small grouping is highly important, therefore in my classroom, you'll see lots of grouping.

When asked about examples of highly effective teaching she has observed in other classrooms, Ms. Manning replied, "I see a lot of energy and great classroom management." She clarified, "When I say management, it doesn't necessarily mean discipline; it means the structure of the classroom in which kids take charge. They know what to do. They've been trained and it's been well organized." Again, Ms. Manning referred to energy and caring when asked how she thinks students would define a highly effective teacher. She commented, "They want to see energy and a caring attitude." She added, "They want to have a voice and for learning to be fun. Students of all ages want to talk and with guidance from the teacher they can direct their own learning. I've been told many times by students that my class is fun."

Knowledge, Experiences, and Factors

Regarding factors that have contributed most to her development as a highly effective teacher, Ms. Manning immediately credited professional development opportunities as a career-changing event. In particular, she referred to multiple conferences pertaining to Singapore Math [math teaching method based on concrete, pictorial, and abstract steps]. She professed:

> I always thought I was a good math teacher, but through training and professional development, my teaching style changed significantly. One of my former principals gave me opportunities to attend several conferences with Singapore Math. It really changed my perspective. I feel like I was learning an in depth learning, common core-like. It was a huge part of my development as a teacher. I used to be a traditional teacher who taught straight from the book so it highlighted for me new concepts and strategies for teaching, trying to find that in-depth understanding for my students versus just brushing the surface in just looking

at basic computation. I think it's an emphasis on in-depth understanding in which kids are allowed to go through the concrete to visual to abstract stages versus going straight to the abstract stage and not allowing kids to see the whole process through and having that understanding that they see when they get the visual.

When asked which individual(s) contributed to her development as a highly effective teacher, Ms. Manning offered, "Probably number one is my former principal." She emphatically stated, "She was my inspiration as a leader and as a friend." She elaborated:

> She allowed me to be myself, but yet still kind of kept that push. She set higher expectations for me and noticed that I'm not one to fail so she gave me good suggestions in a positive way and again, she had a belief in me because she gave me all these opportunities. She knew I was the type of person who would take advantage of the opportunities and use them to me and my student's advantage. I like that she has a backbone. We didn't always agree on every theory, but yet I like the fact that she stood strongly in what she believed in, but was the first to admit she was wrong if it didn't come out like she expected. I really respect that in a leader.

Ms. Manning also spoke about her father as an inspiration to enter the teaching profession. She expressed:

As a child, I watched my father as a teacher. He was a huge inspiration. Hearing his students talk about him made me want that same thing. Maybe that was a part of me becoming a teacher. I wanted that affirmation and a part of something that he was such a huge part of. He made social studies fun because of his passion for history.

Practices and Methods

When asked about preparing high quality and rigorous lesson plans in terms of setting instructional outcomes, Ms. Manning referred to her "theory on highly effective teaching" She expounded on her theory and explained in detail her planning process:

> My lesson plans revolve around my students being the leaders of my classroom. I plan my lessons where it's very little whole group in favor of small grouping. However, it has to be thought out because your lessons and activities have to be constructed where students can take charge and yet have some [teacher] leadership in there with questioning prompts. I train my students on the questioning techniques through my own modeling and I have questioning cards to help with things like that. By the end of the year, they didn't need those questioning prompts.
>
> My main focus is engagement with organization and structure coming from my part. In the perfect world, I developed the unit first. I did pretesting because I did

differentiated instruction. Therefore, I needed the pretest to tell me what my groups were. Teaching math, you can't formulate your groups from the beginning of the year testing. I may have had someone who was great at algebra, but when it came to geometry needed to change groups. Pretesting was a huge part of lesson planning. After the pretest, I based my timeline on what was needed. I usually referenced ten to twenty minutes per day for whole group, a daily instruction to introduce the overall concept, then we broke out into sessions. I unit planned, but my unit plans with the weekly plans changed often depending on what the week's outcomes looked like.

When I asked Ms. Manning to describe her daily classroom routines and procedures, she emphasized the importance of continuous engagement and her role as a facilitator. She reasoned and elucidated:

From the minute they walk in, besides the greeting I give them, it's important to begin with engagement. I knew if I didn't have a task waiting for them, it would take five to ten minutes to get them on task when I was ready. Something right then and there as soon as they walk in is key. After they did a daily activity, then we would begin the whole group type of discussion. Even though I was teaching in front of the class, I was always engaging my students with questioning, getting feedback from them. Often times, students would take over that whole group part and then break into small group stations during which I would pull students in small groups to give them what they needed based on that pretest.

In my classroom, I was more of a facilitator. My students took charge from the time they walked in. I had a job for every student. I never picked up technology or other resource and materials. The jobs change. You know there's certain jobs for certain students based on their uniqueness. My class was structured so that it was completely student centered in which they had control. They liked it. They felt more accountable. It took pressure off of me. My kids were probably more tired than I was at the end of our class.

Ms. Manning claimed that she uses Bloom's Taxonomy when developing lesson plans in order to orchestrate high-level questioning and discussion. She explained:

I always utilize through Blooms [Taxonomy], questioning prompts that would not just help me, but would help the students question each other. I modeled and then had questioning prompts which I called talking cards at the tables all the time. When the students got a little lost when talking with each other, they could flip through the cards to help move the discussion along. This was every day, all day. Questioning was a huge part of my classroom. I use the talking cards, not because I needed them but for modeling for them. Through modeling, we did open versus

close ended questions just to see the difference between the
two.

Ms. Manning acknowledged the significance of respectful
redirection and the importance of outcome-based activities to
ensure that all students are engaged. She illustrated:

With students working in stations, I can look up and
monitor their engagement. With some students, you need
to be sure that when they're active, they're actually working
on the content. I had a work plan that we called artifacts.
As they rotated through their stations, there were several
artifacts they had to produce which is a major component
of Bloom's Taxonomy. Through their creation of artifacts,
they were able to show to me their level of understanding
of the concept. Those [artifacts] were turned in at the end
of the week on which a scoring rubric was used.

Just flowing through the room, spot-checking, listening in
on conversations helps to formatively monitor their
learning. They rarely got off task because I was the type of
teacher who showed that level of compassion and with my
understanding, it wouldn't take much to get them back on
task. When they did get off task or distracted another
student, most of the time, it would only take "that look." I
would squat down to their level, speak softly into their ear
reminding them about how important it is for them to stay
on task, and that the time in my classroom is to be used so
that they can better their ability. That worked almost all the

time to keep them or get them back on track.

In a discussion regarding assessment and monitoring student learning, Ms. Manning accentuated the importance of measuring growth and content mastery. She explained:

> I started pre assessments about five years ago and realized the importance of those because of the small grouping. Through the pre assessments, I knew that small grouping would change throughout the year as different students had different strengths and weaknesses. I informally assess a lot. I do a lot of spot checking, walking around, questioning.
>
> As far as formal assessments, I use Eagle [online assessment instrument] or some other online resource to formulate those tests. Those were done in advance to lesson planning and instruction. My unit assessments were the summative assessments. My pre- and post-tests looked similar if not identical. I needed to know where they were in the pre-test and then measure their growth level on the post test. There is always an opportunity to retest. It's not about grades, it's about understanding. I wanted the grade to reflect their true level of understanding. My students were very clear about having the opportunity to improve; they just needed to work towards that.

Support Systems

When asked about how her administrator(s) prepared her for the Compass observations, Ms. Manning replied, "We had a pre observation meeting in which we went over the expectations. We went over my lesson plan. We discussed it." She added:

> Both administrators gave me suggestions. They wanted me to elaborate a little more in some areas at times. I think it was great leadership on their part. It wasn't that they disagreed with what I was doing; they just wanted to make sure that I had all of the components adequately addressed.

When reflecting on the observation experience, Ms. Manning said, "It was beneficial because I used that fall observation as an opportunity to change what I needed in the spring to make sure I stayed at the highly effective level. I was able to use their feedback to improve on my spring lesson planning."

Regarding what she needed from local and state levels of education in order to maintain highly effectiveness, Ms. Manning declared:

> We need more professional development and training as we transition to common core math and in particular, with EngageNY [curriculum resource] and Eureka Math [curriculum resource]. It's so open to interpretation. I'd like to be more unified in our district which will take more training at both the district and state levels.

She concluded by offering, "I like accountability. I like evaluation. I like the Danielson rubric. I like knowing what's expected of me."

14. MS. MURRAY

Ms. Murray has been in education for nine years with the first eight as a classroom teacher. She's taught English, math, science and social studies at the third and fourth grade levels. She is currently employed as an instructional coach at an elementary school with one section of fourth grade math remediation. She obtained her bachelor's degree from a regional university in southwest Louisiana and her master's degree from an accredited online university. Ms. Murray is certified to teach regular education grades first through fifth. The school at which she taught during the 2013-2014 school year is located in an urban area where 95% of the student population qualified for free or reduced lunch. She draws from her previous career in finance as a means of connecting her math lessons and activities to real world applications.

Definition of Highly Effective Teaching

Ms. Murray defined a highly effective teacher as one who "actively engages his or her students in learning at all times." She pointed out that the Danielson rubric clearly identified what was needed to earn a highly effective rating. She especially appreciated the constructivism approach of the rubric in which "students lead and teachers facilitate the learning environment." She recognized the importance of struggling as part of the learning experience and elucidated:

> It's important to be a facilitator and able to let go. I've only been teaching for nine years and it has drastically changed from teachers doing all the talking while formatively assessing their body language to now, students are being asked to produce a product or explain their thinking or work with a partner. Effective planning through execution is key, but you have to be flexible. You can plan a beautiful lesson but with kids, you never know where you're going to have to go. What happens on that Monday may force you to either scrap your plans for that week and do them all over or slightly modify them. I heard a powerful quote a few years ago and it didn't mean anything to me until we started using the Danielson rubric..."If the students are not struggling, they're not learning." Before, you didn't want your students to struggle. There was a misconception that if they struggled, it meant there was something I wasn't doing right, but now I realize that the struggle is needed for real learning to occur.

Ms. Murray offered a rich description of a facilitated classroom compared to a more traditional instructional approach:

You'll see the students doing a lot without the teacher telling them. From the beginning, the students will take the initiative to mark themselves present, then students will note when other students are absent. When it's time to transition, the students will take that lead. The teacher will step back. Students are in control of most of what's going on in the classroom. The teacher will step in only when and where it's needed to get them back on track. You notice certain things posted around the room. For example, learning outcomes are posted, not just objectives, because objectives can last for weeks. When a student walks in and sees that, it helps them begin with the end in mind. You'll see the student's agenda and posters to help them self-assess or peer assess.

When asked how she thought her students would define a highly effective teacher, she offered, "A teacher who is a pusher with high expectations and communicates those expectations to the students. Although," she continued, "not every student will have the same expectations." Ms. Murray then referred to the importance of creating a fun learning environment from the student's perspective. She explained:

Be goofy, fun, be human. When I make mistakes, I let them know it's okay to correct me. When I was young, you never corrected the teacher. I let them know that I make mistakes too. I'm fun. I love science and math. All of my lessons are hands-on or connected to the real world. I came from a business world. I worked at a bank for ten years with a business management degree.

When Ms. Manning entered the education profession, she "believed what the children lacked was why they needed to know things." She continued, "All of this stuff connects. It's going somewhere. They're going to use it later."

Knowledge, Experiences, and Factors

When asked about factors that have contributed most to her development as a highly effective teacher, Ms. Murray credited the support she has at school and experiences in the Teacher Advancement Program (TAP) early in her teaching career. She commented:

> We've had a lead teacher who was a tremendous help. Being able to go to her and ask her to research new techniques and then model it for you and your students was invaluable. When I came into teaching, our school was under the TAP [Teacher Advancement Program] initiative. I attribute all of my effectiveness to TAP. I receive a lot of support from administrators. My room is full of boxes of technology, resources, and materials. My principal takes in a wish list of whatever you think you can use in your classroom and gets most, if not all, you need.

When asked about significant events that have contributed to her teaching success, Ms. Murray referred to her previous non-education career. She stated:

My financial background has helped. I love math and I always have loved math and science. It [previous career] helps me to connect with the real world when I come into my classroom.

Another significant event was the Math and Science Partnerships program funded by a federal grant. It's three summers long that included a month's worth of us learning, getting information from college professors, really digging deep into the curriculum. Every summer was a unique focus. We dug so deep into it that when I came into my classroom, I had a better, deeper understanding of the math I was teaching.

Practices and Methods

Ms. Murray described the following procedure regarding preparing high quality and rigorous lesson plans in terms of setting instructional outcomes:

First, go to the standards. They drive the instruction. I always start with my assessment piece first. From my assessment and tasks, that's how I plan my lesson so I'll know how high to hit. It's very important to start with those standards first, but not just with your grade level standards because if they master those, you've got to be ready to dive into the next grade level standards.

When I asked Ms. Murray to describe her classroom routines and procedures, she started by mentioning that she's "never had an issue with discipline." She claimed, "My principal wonders why we never send kids to the office." She was raised in a high poverty community, similar to that of her students, and therefore she understands the challenges her students face at home. She expounded:

> A lot of these children don't have love and compassion at home, so I make sure that every morning, no matter what's going on, I meet them at my door with a smile on my face and a hug. They all have my cell phone number so if they had any issues the night before, they can call me. I'll help them with their homework so they know that there's someone who cares about them and their success at school. Children know and can tell that you care. Whatever you establish and put in place on day one, they'll continue with it.
>
> We have a reward system in place. I like to drink water throughout the day. Well, if I'm going to do it, I'll allow them to do it. If they want to bring water or a snack, they can bring it, but it teaches them responsibility. I never had an issue with wanting to go to the bathroom during class or trash on the floor. They know if they do those things, I'll take that privilege away. It's that mutual respect. Letting them know that I'm human. I mess up. I make mistakes. They want to respect you.

Ms. Murray then proceeded to share her methods of dealing with those rare occasions when students did not meet classroom expectations. She explained that she doesn't have classroom rules;

instead she has a "discipline cycle." She displayed a small stack of laminated cards and said:

If a student gets off task or is doing something like talking during instruction, the "1" card goes on their desk. That's a non-verbal warning to get on task. After a while, if they got back on task with no further issues, I'd pick it up and place a different card on their desk which thanked them for positive behavior. If they didn't get back on task, I'd flip the one to a two, get in their ear and tell them, "If you continue to disrupt the class, then you're going to choose from the negative consequences menu." It wasn't my choice. It was their choice. That removes the teacher from the negative consequence process and makes it less personal.

They also fill out a reflection form that goes in their folder and a copy goes home to the parents. That process kept them out of the office. By giving them that choice, it was like being a little adult in the classroom. So simple. Yet so effective. That's modeling how important it is to not distract the class.

Orchestrating high-level questioning and discussion is a strategy in which Ms. Murray uses "a lot of different resources" including ideas she finds on Pinterest [social network sharing website]. She uses "a Kagan questioning card" as well as "a flip chart with Bloom's taxonomy to help me development my questions." She expounded:

I let the students ask the questions. I plan for questioning to make sure that I hit all the points. Accountable talk anchors are on a poster for reference. They're used to answering, not asking questions, so the poster helps to initialize their questions. When they answer, they can't just say "yes or no." They have to continue by saying, "because" and then refer to a text-based source to support their answer. After they refer to the text, then they can refer to a personal experience.

When asked how she ensures that all students are engaged, Ms. Murray expressed that she has success with managing small groups and technology-based stations at which the students receive immediate feedback. With various software programs, she is able to monitor student progress and determine which students need one-on-one assistance. She explained, "At the end of the day, I can pull the reports for planning purposes the next day. I can see who needs extra time or extra help on different skills with an individual task card or stay on the regular task card." She emphasized, "That's how you ensure you don't leave any students behind. And software that gives them immediate feedback and data that I can use to monitor their mastery of content."

In a discussion regarding assessment and monitoring student learning, Ms. Murray stated, "I ask a lot of questions and they ask a lot of questions." She initially mentioned an emphasis on self-assessment:

When they come up to present or explain their work, they

also can rate themselves. When they fill out an exit ticket, it'll tell me their level of understanding according to their own perception. They rate themselves.

Ms. Murray then explained her methods and theory of student assessment in terms of content mastery. She illustrated:

When they go to stations, I use the data I'm able to pull up to determine grades. I have student conferences, just me sitting one on one with a student during their PE time. I work with Coach. It's very organized and it only takes about four minutes per student. We do that every two weeks. It's just an individual check in.

Support Systems

When asked how her administrator(s) prepared her for the Compass observations, Ms. Murray chuckled and then replied, "Well, we didn't have much preparation. We were all clueless, so I prepared myself. I actually bought my own book by Danielson to prepare myself." She continued, "I think when the rubric first came out, a lot of people were just guessing at what the rubric meant, so I got that book and studied it." She also noted that she consulted with a teacher friend who taught at a different school who "helped to understand what they'd be looking for." When reflecting on the observation experience, Ms. Murray said, "With the pre-observation conference, I was able to make my evaluator aware of situations in my room such as students who have unique or special needs." She elaborated:

I'm able to explain to him why I may focus more on one or two students. I'd rather get observed unannounced, but the preconference works because it gives me an opportunity to explain what he'll probably see and why. The post-observation conference gives you that immediate feedback. I don't care how highly effective you are. There's always something I can do a little bit better.

What I like about our evaluators, he told me, "What I saw was this, but if you did this one thing, it would bring you from here to here." He takes the time to go through it. He even records it on his iPad so he's able to point out, "If you would have done this..." If you stop growing, something's wrong. You get that refinement and you know where to go from there. Don't just tell me this is my issue and not offer a solution.

Upon reflecting on what she needed from local and state levels of education in order to maintain highly effectiveness, Ms. Murray declared, "We need professional development that is meaningful, not just for the sake of having it." She reasoned:

A lot of times, we'll go to meetings that have nothing to do with anything important. Just get the information from us. Let us fill out a survey to see what kind of professional development we want and need. We should get to select professional development that meets our unique needs, not just a one size fits all. For example, not everyone needs more training on differentiated instruction. Some may need more training on questioning. Some teachers need more training with unpacking the standards. We need quality training that's differentiated for teachers.

She concluded, "Get input from teachers on what type of training we need. Let that come from the teachers, not top down. Just like we differentiate for students, practice what you preach."

15. SUMMARY OF MAJOR FINDINGS

The major findings of this research are presented by research question. Research Question One sought to define highly effective teaching. Emergent themes included:

- fun, interesting, meaningful activities,
- high level of teacher energy, enthusiasm,
- high expectations,
- emphasis on high order thinking skills,
- consistent, student-led routines, structured, organized classroom, and
- caring, compassionate, empathetic, positive attitude, fair, good rapport with students

Research Question Two sought to identify the characteristics, factors, and events that led to highly effective teaching. Emergent themes included:

- pre-teaching, non-education life experiences,
- gaining deeper knowledge of content through professional development and independent research,

- mentors who provided guidance, inspiration,
- sharing ideas and best practices with colleagues through social networking, and
- personal reflection.

Research Question Three sought to identify the practices and methods of highly effective teaching. Emergent themes included:

- lesson planning strategies,
- student engagement, meaningful activities,
- questioning and discussion techniques,
- classroom management routines, expectations, procedures, and
- assessment of content mastery and as a guideline for remediation.

Research Question Four sought to identify support systems that contributed to highly effective teaching. Emergent themes included:

- clear understanding of the observation rubric,
- effective communication/planning with observers prior to observation, and immediate observation feedback.

16. CONCLUSIONS

The study investigated the characteristics, practices and experiences of teachers with perfect evaluation ratings. Findings from the study suggest the overall conclusion that the likelihood of teachers earning a highly effective evaluation rating increases when teachers exhibit all or most of the following, (a) genuinely compassionate and caring, (b) plan lessons according to standards, (c) incorporate meaningful, interesting and high order thinking activities in their lessons, (d) facilitate a well-organized and student-centered classroom, (e) possess a deep understanding of content knowledge, and (f) assess for content mastery with remediation opportunities. Related conclusions include the importance of a clear understanding of the observation expectations as laid forth in the observation rubric.

Genuine compassion and caring of a teacher towards students is consistent with the effective teacher research of Kottler and Zehm (2000) and Stronge (2002) who asserted that genuinely caring about students both academically and personally was crucial to the students' academic success. Research findings from the study also affirm the necessity of a well-organized classroom (Sammons, 2006; Stronge, 2002). Stronge (2002) particularly noted the importance of maximizing instructional time via effective classroom management and organization. Among the emergent themes is the significance of teacher preparation which is consistent with the research of Darling-Hammond (2006). Darling-Hammond specifically noted that knowledge of teaching methodology and subject content matter are leading factors in teacher effectiveness. The importance of assessing for content mastery with remediation opportunities is in agreement with research by Stronge (2002), Sartain, Stoelinga, and Brown (2011), and Grant, Stronge, and Popp (2008). Furthermore, the positive impact of incorporating meaningful, interesting, and higher order thinking activities in effective teacher lessons is in agreement with research by Muijs and Reynolds (2002).

17. IMPLICATIONS FOR PRACTICE

One of the most significant challenges for all schools is to have an effective teacher in every classroom (Rice, 2003). Findings from the study suggest that there are commonalities among highly effective teachers in terms of characteristics, practices, and experiences. Suggestions for increasing the number and quality of effective teachers in classrooms follow.

Effective teachers.

Teachers who aspire to either become effective or increase their effectiveness must possess an inherent trait of genuine caring and compassion for the students they teach. Noddings (2005) explained that teachers caring for their well-being is what mattered most to students. Teachers must also be willing to establish a positive rapport with their students by being fair, praise and recognize effort and achievement, be attentive to student emotional needs, promote and model mutual respect and develop senses of humor and humility. Ghiora (2010) suggested that students described effective teachers as those who were fair and just and didn't give unfair advantages to some students. Borich (2000) indicated that students identified effective teachers as those who used meaningful verbal praise to actively engage students in the learning process.

According to McDermott and Rothenberg (2000), students preferred teachers with a sense of humor and found those teachers made learning enjoyable. According to Irvine and Armento (2001), students defined caring teachers as those who set high expectations, provided a structured learning environment with clear limits, and pushed them to achieve. Additionally, effective teachers should continuously seek learning opportunities through independent research, social network sharing of ideas and professional development opportunities provided by administration. Stronge (2002) found that effective teachers displayed a commitment to both ongoing professional development and student learning. Stronge continued by adding, "Effective teachers learn and grow as they expect their students to learn and grow. They serve as powerful examples of lifelong learners as they find ways to develop professionally" (p. 20).

Effective teacher preparation and professional development.

Colleges of education and teacher certification agencies should continue to focus on the findings of research geared towards identifying teacher effectiveness. Darling-Hammond (2006) indicated that teacher preparation (knowledge of teaching and learning), subject matter knowledge, experience, and the combined set of qualifications measured by teacher licensure are all leading factors in teacher effectiveness. Teacher preparation programs for future teachers and professional development opportunities for current teachers should prioritize training in constructing a classroom environment that is structured, organized and student-centered. Future and current teachers need to understand the importance of creating a classroom atmosphere of high expectations and continuous student engagement from bell to bell. Furthermore, teachers must learn how to facilitate lessons that include meaningful activities with high order thinking questioning, discovery and discussion. Potential and current teachers should also be eminently familiar with how to effectively assess student learning with an emphasis on content mastery, immediate feedback and remediation opportunities.

Administration.

Lastly, school- and district-level leadership should assist teachers in becoming more effective by providing them with meaningful, relevant and professional development opportunities tailored to their specific needs. It is vitally important for administrators to clearly communicate teacher expectations as they relate to the observation rubric. Administrators should regularly ensure that rigorous, student-centered lessons with meaningful, high order thinking activities are in place. They should provide immediate, helpful feedback that promotes a productive, solutions-based atmosphere during post-observation conferences. School leaders should also consider facilitating a mentoring process in which ineffective or less effective teachers have access to highly effective teachers in terms of viewing and modeling best practices. School leaders would also be encouraged to create opportunities for highly effective teachers to observe and work with less effective teachers in an effort to provide constructive feedback to them.

The results of the study and related research can provide school leaders with a list of favorable characteristics, practices and traits to use as part of the hiring and interview process. It is recommended that administrators incorporate the study's research questions during the interview process in order to compare answers of applicants to those of the study's participating highly effective teachers. The Wallace Foundation (2013) believed principals can no longer function simply as building managers; rather, they have to be, or become, instructional leaders who are proficient in the hiring process, conducting classroom observations and providing meaningful professional development opportunities.

18. CONCLUDING REMARKS

The study provided insight into the characteristics, practices, and experiences of teachers who earned a perfect teacher evaluation rating. The ten teachers in the study passionately described who they are as teachers, how they manage their classrooms, their instructional practices, as well as the people, trainings and various experiences that have led to their professional success. Each appeared to be confident in their teaching abilities yet humble of their accomplishments.

One of the most compelling findings of this study is the characteristic of caring. While speaking with them, it became apparent that each teacher possessed a natural trait of genuinely caring for their students. They expressed caring in a variety of ways including encouraging pats on the back as well as spending hours outside the classroom preparing lessons with meaningful activities to grading papers until the wee hours of the morning in order to provide vital immediate feedback. All of the teachers alluded to recognizing, protecting, and nurturing a productive level of mutual respect. Each of the participants exuded the impression of being organized, firm yet compassionate, confident, content knowledgeable and internally motivated to continuously seek new and better instructional methods and practices.

Through all of my years involved in education as a student, parent of students, teacher, teacher of teachers and school administrator, I had internally defined what I thought a highly effective teacher should be. The findings of this study affirmed my beliefs. There have been numerous studies conducted with the purpose of defining effective teaching. However, I'm convinced that a handful of K-12 students with no prior knowledge of the reviewed literature could have provided a list of characteristics and practices of their definition of a highly effective teacher similar or identical to the findings in this and other related studies.

There is no magic pill, no one particular professional development workshop, and no one particular type of pre-service program that will guarantee highly effective teaching. Highly effective teachers are not simply born. Teachers who possess a genuinely high level of caring and compassion for their students, but lack content knowledge, structure, organizational skills, and effective instructional methods will most likely not be deemed "highly effective" by any measurement. In contrast, students whose teachers possess superior content knowledge, structure, and organizational skills, but do not have a positive rapport with them will not likely put forth their best effort, especially on non-high stakes standardized tests. Ultimately, teachers who genuinely care for their students by both possessing a sincere concern of their well-being and by implementing best practices will be successful and highly effective.

References

Borich, G. D. (2000). Effective Teaching Methods (4 ed.). New Jersey: Prentice- Hall,Inc.

Darling-Hammond, L. (2006). Powerful teacher education: Lessons from exemplary   programs. San Francisco: John Wiley and Sons, Inc.

Ghiora, W. (2010, July 3). Teaching for a Change: Characteristics of Effective Teachers. Retrieved December 10, 2013, from http://teaching4achange.blogspot.com/2010/07/characteristics-of-effective-teachers.html

Grant, L., Stronge, J. H., & Popp, P. A. (2008). Effective teaching and at-risk/highly mobile students: What do award-winning teachers do? Case studies of award-winning teachers of at risk/highly mobile students. Retrieved June 30, 2008 from: http://www.serve.org/nche/downloads/eff_teach.pdf.

Irvine, J. J. & Armento, B. J. (2001). Culturally Responsive Teaching: Lesson Planning for Elementary and Middle Grades. New York, New York: The McGraw Hill Companies, Inc.

Kottler, J. A., & Zehm, S. J. (2000). *One being a teacher* (2nd ed.). Corwin Press, Inc

McDermott and Rothenberg. (2000). *The Characteristics of Effective Teachers in High Poverty Schools: Triangulating our data*. Paper presented at the Annual Meeting of the American Educational Research Association, New Orleans.

Muijs, D., & Reynolds, D. (2002). Teachers' beliefs and behaviors: What really matters? Journal of classroom interaction, 2, 3-15.

Noddings, N. (2005). Caring in education, the encyclopedia of informal education. Retrieved from www.infed.org/biblio/noddings_caring_in_education.htm.

Rice, J. K. (2003). *Teacher quality: Understanding the effectiveness of teacher attributes*. Washington, DC: Economic Policy Institute.

Sammons, P. (2006), The Contribution of International Studies on Educational Effectiveness: Current and future directions, Educational Research and Evaluation, Vol. 12, No.6, December 2006, pp. 583-593. Sanders, W.L. (1998). Value-added assessment. *The School Administrator, 55*(11), 24-32.

Sartain, L., Stoelinga, S. R., & Brown, E. R. (2011). *Rethinking teacher evaluation in Chicago: Lessons learned from classroom observations, principal- teacher   conferences, and district implementation*. Chicago, IL: Consortium on Chicago School Research at the University of Chicago.

Stronge, J. H. (2002). *Qualities of effective teachers*. Alexandria, VA: Association for Supervision and Curriculum Development.

The Wallace Foundation. (2013). The school principal as leader: Guiding schools to better teaching and learning. New York, NY: Retrieved December 15, 2013, from
http://www.wallacefoundation.org/knowledge-center/school-leadership/effective principal-leadership/Documents/The-School-Principal-as-Leader-Guiding-Schools-to Better-Teaching-and-Learning-2nd-Ed.pdf

ABOUT THE AUTHOR

Dr. Keith E. Leger earned his Doctorate degree in Educational Leadership from Lamar University in 2014. He received both his Master of Education degree (1997) and Education Specialist degree in Administration and Supervision (1999) from McNeese State University. Dr. Leger earned his Bachelor of Science degree in Kinesiology from Louisiana State University in 1993.

Dr. Leger retired as a School Administrator in 2015 having also served as a Classroom Teacher, District Quality Supervisor, Grant Director and Athletics Coach.

He is a member of the National Beta Club Board of Directors, a lifetime member of Associated Professional Educators of Louisiana (APEL) and an active member of the American Evaluation Association.

Dr. Leger served on the Louisiana Standards Review Steering Committee for English, Math and Science (2015-16) and is serving on the Board of Elementary and Secondary Education Minimum Foundation Program Task Force and the Louisiana Commission on Assessment Review and Use in Public Schools.

Dr. Leger is the owner and manager of High Quality Program Improvement & Evaluation (www.hqpie.com).

Made in the USA
Lexington, KY
20 October 2018